# The whole family Cookbook

# The
# whole family
# Cookbook

**Includes 75+ Recipes to Make Together!**

### Celebrate the Goodness of
### Locally Grown Foods

## Michelle Stern FOUNDER OF What's Cooking
#### Photography by Matthew Carden

Aadamsmedia
Avon, Massachusetts

Published by
Adams Media, a division of F+W Media, Inc.
57 Littlefield Street, Avon, MA 02322. U.S.A.
www.adamsmedia.com

ISBN 10: 1-4405-1120-9
ISBN 13: 978-1-4405-1120-2
eISBN 10: 1-4405-1219-1
eISBN 13: 978-1-4405-1219-3

Printed in China.

10   9   8   7   6   5   4   3   2   1

Library of Congress Cataloging-in-Publication Data is available from the publisher.

Arrows © istockphoto / cajoer
Recycling stamp © istockphoto / MrPlumo
Leaf © istockphoto / KachinTihu
Wooden spoon © istockphoto / duckycards
Jam © istockphoto / TSchon
Handprints © istockphoto / Photo2008

This book is available at quantity discounts for bulk purchases. For information, please call 1-800-289-0963.

To *my* Whole Family—

You have inspired and motivated me.

# Acknowledgments

I could not have written this book without the support of my family, friends, and students. Thank you for having confidence in me, even when my own faltered.

To Amelia and Ari: Thank you for the hours you spent with me in the kitchen, garden, and the farmer's market; for tasting new foods; for learning to clean up our spills; for the hugs you offered when a recipe didn't turn out as expected; and for the love you lavished on me, throughout. It was humbling to see how proud you are of our book, and I hope this has been an experience that you will always remember. Glenn, I am grateful for your appetite and your honesty. Thank you for all of the waffles, crepes, and pancakes you made on Saturday mornings so that I could write, edit, and escape with the dogs.

Recipe Testers (there were more than 80 of you!): I am eternally grateful for your generosity, honesty, and kindness. You found my mistakes, made my recipes easier to follow, and spent quality time with your families as you experimented in the kitchen together on my behalf. This book has been a collaborative effort, and it is my deepest wish that you consider it "ours."

Jennifer and Matthew Carden, photography team and friends extraordinaire: We fought tooth and nail to have your work in my book, and I would do it again in an instant. The fun we had together in the kitchen would have been enough (deyenu!) but the resulting photographs are what make this book shine and make it inspiring. I am blessed to count you as friends and colleagues and love that our history includes this and many other memorable endeavors—all with the goal of feeding families, helping children, and playing with our food.

The pages of this book would be incomplete without the beautiful faces (and hands) of Maia Perry, Mae Gerlach, Faeryn Dunnigan, Ryan Chung, Daniel and Sandra Chavez, and my kids, Amelia and Ari. I am thankful for your adventurous spirits and healthy appetites. And yes, I will try to make this book a "bestseller" so you can "become famous."

*The Whole Family Cookbook* is just that. It was a thrill to include recipes from my great-aunt, Beate Berliner, and from my mom, Susie Stern. Thanks to my dad, Richard, for joining in on the photography fun. While you are usually on the other side of the camera, having you in these photos was a touching image that I'm not likely to forget.

I am grateful to matchmaker (and slow-cooker lady) Stephanie O'Dea, for introducing me to the wonderful agent that we now share, Alison Picard. Thank you both for seeing the value of my work and for encouraging me to work hard to get my message out to families.

Victoria Sandbrook at Adams Media—you had the knack of making me feel comfortable, even as I navigated through the mysterious waters of writing my first book. I appreciated your humor and patience as you waded through my endless questions, and am grateful that you were always able to ground me and calm my anxious nerves.

Wendy Simard at Adams Media—you waved your wordsmith wand over this manuscript and sprinkled it with a dusting of positive reinforcement. Your comments were helpful and kind and gave my confidence a boost at the tail end of this exhilarating process.

To Mary Pryor and Maria Grey, two of my oldest friends: Although we were never infused with school spirit in our younger years, I count you as two of the best cheer-leaders my team could ever ask for!

# Contents

Introduction
**Raising Little Locavores / 1**

**Chapter 1**
**Ready, Set, Go!**
**Engaging Kids in the Kitchen / 5**

Recipe for Cooking with Toddlers . . . . . . . . 8

**Chapter 2**
**Breakfast of Champions / 13**

Mini Frittatas . . . . . . . . . . . . . . . . . . . . . 14
Breakfast Anytime Pizza . . . . . . . . . . . . . 15
Yummy Strawberry Yogurt Parfait . . . . . . . 18
Banana Sunshine Smoothie. . . . . . . . . . . 20
Sweet and Salty Glazed Bacon . . . . . . . . 21
Corny Raspberry Muffins. . . . . . . . . . . . . 22
Baked Apple Puff. . . . . . . . . . . . . . . . . . . 24
Steel-Cut Oatmeal with Dates . . . . . . . . . 26
Sweet Potato Biscuits . . . . . . . . . . . . . . . 28
Breakfast Burrito . . . . . . . . . . . . . . . . . . . 30
Grilled Cheese with Nutella . . . . . . . . . . . 35
Crunchy Granola . . . . . . . . . . . . . . . . . . . 37

**Chapter 3**
**Lunchtime Favorites / 39**

A-B-C Frittata. . . . . . . . . . . . . . . . . . . . . 40
Wrap It Up: BBQ Style . . . . . . . . . . . . . . 44

Squashed Sweet Potato Soup. . . . . . . . . . 45
Wrap It Up: L'egg-o Style. . . . . . . . . . . . . 48
Thai Spring Rolls . . . . . . . . . . . . . . . . . . 49
Smashed Avocado on Toast . . . . . . . . . . . 52
Chinese Chicken Salad . . . . . . . . . . . . . . 53
There's Turkey in My Pocket . . . . . . . . . . . 55
R & B Chili . . . . . . . . . . . . . . . . . . . . . . . 56
Croque Monsieur . . . . . . . . . . . . . . . . . . . 58
Wrap It Up: Toga Style. . . . . . . . . . . . . . . 60
Chewy Maple Granola Bars. . . . . . . . . . . . 61
Salty Pretzel Pillows. . . . . . . . . . . . . . . . . 63

**Chapter 4**
**What's for Dinner? / 67**

Chicken Piccata with Linguine. . . . . . . . . . 68
Minestrone with White Beans and Kale. . . . 71
Pork Ribs with Asian BBQ Sauce . . . . . . . 74
Grandma's Spaghetti Gravy. . . . . . . . . . . . 77
Biscuit-Topped Chicken Potpie . . . . . . . . . 79
Wish-for-a-Fish Pasta . . . . . . . . . . . . . . . 82
Pork Chops with Sage Butter. . . . . . . . . . . 84
Sorrel-icious Sole. . . . . . . . . . . . . . . . . . . 86
Greek Shrimp with Feta . . . . . . . . . . . . . . 88
Summertime Kabobs with
Udon Noodles . . . . . . . . . . . . . . . . . . . . . 90
Taco Salad . . . . . . . . . . . . . . . . . . . . . . . 94

Acorn Squash and Wild Rice Bowls . . . . . . .96

Falling for Fall Quesadillas . . . . . . . . . . . . .98

Pumpkin Ravioli . . . . . . . . . . . . . . . . . . . .101

Miso-Glazed Salmon . . . . . . . . . . . . . . . .103

Crispy Tofu Triangles with
Asian Dipping Sauce . . . . . . . . . . . . . . . .104

Turkey Toes . . . . . . . . . . . . . . . . . . . . . .106

Pretzel-Coated Chicken . . . . . . . . . . . . . .108

## Chapter 5
## Scrumptious Sides / 110

Kale Chips . . . . . . . . . . . . . . . . . . . . . . . .111

Potato Latkes . . . . . . . . . . . . . . . . . . . . . .112

Carrot-Raisin Salad . . . . . . . . . . . . . . . . .114

Couscous Salad with Apricots,
Ginger, and Pine Nuts . . . . . . . . . . . . . . .116

Roasted Asparagus . . . . . . . . . . . . . . . . .117

Lemon-Grilled Artichokes
with Garlic Aioli . . . . . . . . . . . . . . . . . . . .118

Mediterranean Quinoa Salad . . . . . . . . . .120

Oven-Fried Zucchini Sticks . . . . . . . . . . .122

Israeli Couscous Salad with
Summer Vegetables . . . . . . . . . . . . . . . . .124

Patriotic Fruit Salad . . . . . . . . . . . . . . . . .126

Spaghetti Squash Two Ways . . . . . . . . . .127

Mashed Sweet Potatoes with
Caramelized Apples . . . . . . . . . . . . . . . . .128

Roasted Broccoli with Lemon . . . . . . . . . .130

Green Salad with Pears, Walnuts,
and Feta . . . . . . . . . . . . . . . . . . . . . . . . .131

Purple Rice . . . . . . . . . . . . . . . . . . . . . . .132

Step-on-the-Gas Baked Beans . . . . . . . .134

## Chapter 6
## Mom-Approved Treats / 136

Stick 'em Up: Frozen Choco Bananas . . . .137

Sweet and Crunchy Strawberry Cups . . . .139

Lemon Buttermilk Sherbet . . . . . . . . . . . .141

Simple Summer Frozen Yogurt . . . . . . . .143

Peaches and Cream Cobbler . . . . . . . . . .144

Cinnamon Pear Clafouti . . . . . . . . . . . . . .147

Apple Crisp with Vanilla Sauce . . . . . . . .148

Chocolate Chip Pumpkin Bread . . . . . . . .150

Coconut Macaroons . . . . . . . . . . . . . . . .152

Cherry Chocolate Chip Cookies . . . . . . .154

Flourless Chocolate Cake . . . . . . . . . . . .156

Luscious Lemon Curd Tartlets . . . . . . . . .158

Nutella Lace Cookies . . . . . . . . . . . . . . . .161

## Chapter 7
## Make Your Own! / 162

Butter . . . . . . . . . . . . . . . . . . . . . . . . . . .163

Pancake Mix . . . . . . . . . . . . . . . . . . . . . .165

Fresh Basil Pesto . . . . . . . . . . . . . . . . . .166

Hummus . . . . . . . . . . . . . . . . . . . . . . . . .168

Puréed Pumpkin . . . . . . . . . . . . . . . . . . .169

Spice Rub Mix . . . . . . . . . . . . . . . . . . . . .170

Hot Cocoa Mix . . . . . . . . . . . . . . . . . . . .171

## Appendix
## Tips for Teachers—
## Cooking in the Classroom / 174

## Seasonal Recipe Index / 176
## Index / 177

# Introduction

# Raising Little Locavores

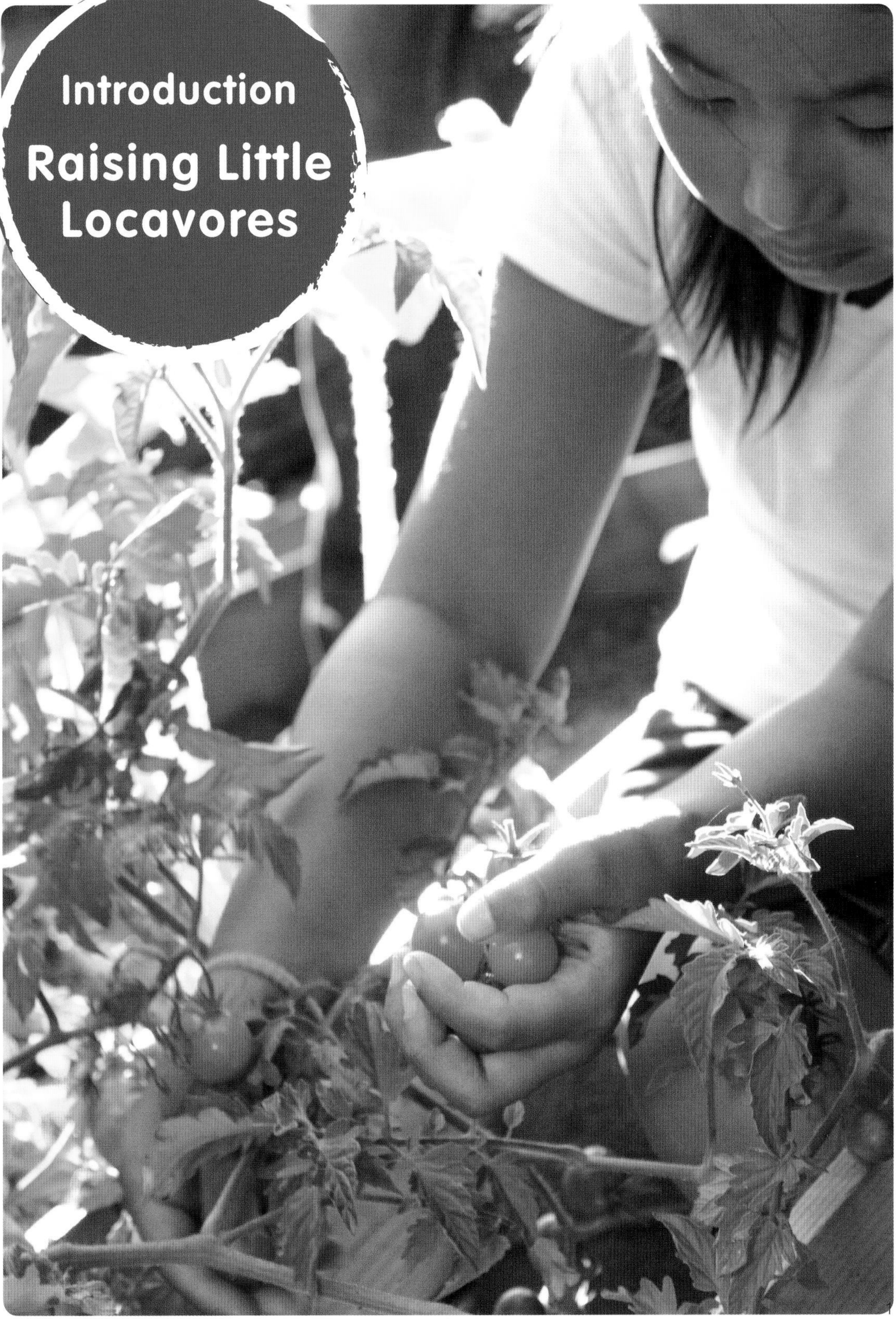

Parenting is a hefty responsibility. It's up to us to teach our children about good manners, how to stay safe, and how to grow up to be independent and confident adults. It's also important that we inspire our kids to make nutritious choices and be good stewards for the earth. Take advantage of teachable moments, such as when shopping for food, because the example you set will help your kids develop a healthy and holistic attitude toward eating that will serve them well throughout their lives!

## First Stop, the Grocery Store

With literally thousands of products vying for your attention at the store, buying food can feel like a daunting task. Some food products aren't even made out of real ingredients. Others travel around the globe to reach your plate, causing pollution and requiring lots of packaging and padding so they don't arrive dented and damaged. Still other foods are grown or processed with herbicides, pesticides, added hormones, and preservatives. If you pay attention (which can be difficult if you have a cranky toddler in tow), you can find foods and artisan products that are made naturally, as they were a hundred years ago. And even better yet, you can find foods that were grown in or near your own community. The best part about that? When you make the conscious choice to buy them, you are not only enjoying delicious, authentic food, you are supporting your local economy at the same time.

Look at the label on your food and take a gander at where it comes from or where it was grown. Do they speak the same language as you? Do an ad hoc geography lesson and see if they are in the same state, country, or hemisphere. If not, it's a pretty clear sign that the food you are eating isn't local.

Another good reason to buy food, of course, is the flavor. But you would probably get busted if the store manager caught you tasting all of the fruits and veggies in the produce section of the grocery store. Not so for the farmer's market—they want you to taste (and love) the food so badly that they cut up samples and put them out on display for your family to try. Do an experiment sometime with your kids—taste one strawberry from every single booth that sells them, and then purchase your booty from the vendor whose fruit tasted the best.

### A Smart Alternative to the Grocery Store

A locavore is someone who tries to eat foods from the local area instead of ones imported from elsewhere. While there are definitely militant locavores around, for the rest of us, it's all about finding balance. Of course it's okay to have chocolate sauce on your vanilla ice cream. Neither chocolate nor vanilla come from your neck of the woods, but maybe the cream in your ice cream comes from a dairy in the next town. The most important factor in becoming a class-act locavore is awareness. Each time your food comes from an area near you, you are making a smaller dent in the environmental impact of the food industry.

## Help Your Family Think Like a Locavore

- **Plant something.** Even if you don't have a patch of earth to your name, you can still plant a pot of herbs to garnish your kitchen window. If you are nervous that your green thumb might actually be a darker shade of black, start small and go with something that is hard to kill—like radishes, herbs, and lettuce. Or let your kids choose what they would like to grow. Give them the responsibility of caring for your new seedlings and watch their pride blossom as their edible plants do the same. Talk about eating locally—it doesn't get better than this!

- **Visit the farmer's market.** Most farmer's markets sell food that was produced within a several-hour drive. When in doubt, ask the vendors how far they came and what their farming practices are. If you are too busy at work or being the social secretary and chauffeur for your children and don't have time to wander the farmer's markets, you can participate in Community Supported Agriculture (CSA). This is a subscription service in which members, in exchange for a small monthly fee, receive a box of fresh, seasonal, and local produce. Some CSAs also have meat available.

- **Take a field trip.** Plan a family day to visit a local farm or a U-Pick location, where you can harvest your own produce. There is nothing like the connection you make with your food when you pick it yourself (dirt under your fingernails and all).

- **Can it.** If you can't imagine your life without the sweetness of peaches or tomatoes, preserve some in jars and save them for later, when they cannot be grown locally. Freezing and dehydrating are also good options for preserving foods.

- **Eat out.** Show your support for the local food movement by eating at restaurants that buy their produce from local farms. Ask the vendors at the farmer's markets which restaurants buy ingredients from them, or call and ask the restaurants where their food comes from.

- **Start small.** Identify a short list of foods that you know you can get locally and begin there. Most regions of the country produce some fruits and veggies, and some even boast a dairy that makes a special variety of cheese.

As a multitasking working parent and child chauffeur, I approach cooking with a realistic and occasionally humorous perspective, and prove that you don't have to be a stay-at-home parent to cook with your kids. *The Whole Family Cookbook* is an approachable, guilt-free book that I hope will inspire you to cook healthy and delicious recipes with your children—and hopefully empower you to consider your environmental impact as you shop and cook with your family.

# Chapter 1

## Ready, Set, Go! Engaging Kids in the Kitchen

Cooking with your kids is a fantastic way to spend time together, and if you are lucky, you will accomplish something productive at the same time! As much as I'd love to visit each of you and spend time with your family in the kitchen, my own kids would miss me too much. So, I'll stick closer to home. But in the meantime, this chapter should help give you some tricks of the trade along with a boost to your self-confidence. You can cook with your kids and develop a healthy relationship to food and the environment along the way.

## Tools of the Trade for Tiny Hands

Over my years in the business of cooking with children, several kitchen gadgets have emerged as favorites. Keep in mind that cooking tools are just that—tools. They are designed to help you in the kitchen and to get the job done. Of course, some will be more appealing to children if they are colorful or come equipped with faces and googly eyes. But try to lean toward function, rather than style. You'll be glad you did—hardly a day goes by that I don't put these items to good use with my children and students!

- **Food chopper:** a great way for kids to release *lots* of energy as they safely pound a plunger that chops food items into bits.

- **Rotary cheese grater:** does more than grate cheese—this little beauty lets kids grate carrots, zucchini, and chocolate, while protecting tender knuckles at the same time.

- **Plastic lettuce knives or metal pumpkin-carving knives:** these child-safe knives are tough enough to saw through carrots, but aren't sharp enough to accidentally cut through skin. The plastic lettuce knife from Oxo and the child-sized knives from Curious Chef are my favorites.

- **Mini-muffin tin:** everything is cuter when it's small! Youngsters will love this pan because it lets them make kid-sized muffins, frittatas, and more.

- **Apple peeler/corer/slicer:** a simple but slightly messy tool that helps little ones (and big ones, alike) peel, core, and slice apples into a long spiral, leaving behind a fun piece of apple-skin spaghetti.

- **Gadgets and gizmos from the Japanese dollar store or Asian market:** they offer molds that press sticky rice and other food into fun shapes!

- **Small scoop:** the perfect partner for the mini-muffin tin, this helps kids get uniform scoops every time. They can also use this for scooping watermelon or teensy balls of ice cream.

- **Colored silicone spatulas:** colorful enough to appeal to kids, but also heat resistant to withstand stirring ingredients in a hot pan.

- **Silicone pastry brush:** what kids wouldn't want to paint their food? Silicone brushes are colorful and heat resistant, and they don't leave little bristles in your food the way traditional pastry brushes do.

- **Scissors:** perfect for snipping fresh herbs or green onions. Reserve a pair of scissors or two just for the kitchen and keep them away from your art projects!

- **Sugar shakers:** the ideal way for kids to sprinkle cinnamon sugar or powdered sugar onto homemade pancakes, French toast, or muffins.

## Beyond Brownies— Palate-Pleasing Offerings

When people discover I teach cooking classes to kids, they assume I must bake a lot of cookies with my students. "How else will you get them to taste what they make?" they wonder aloud.

Is it really that difficult to believe that kids can enjoy good food? I don't mean "good" as in "indulgent." I mean good as in fresh, just-picked, seasonal, and sustainable. I have a lot of firsthand experience that suggests that children who are involved in selecting their food and then help in the kitchen are more likely to eat what they've created. Kids don't need any practice eating cookies and cupcakes. But they *do* need to practice eating their "growing food." Using this phrase is a great way to help kids understand the difference between the food that nourishes them and keeps them healthy and treats that are reserved for special occasions. I use this phrase with kids in my classes and I like it because it explains why those foods are important but doesn't place judgment—talk about positive reinforcement! So why not spend some time creating dishes together that include more fruits and vegetables, or growing food?

Please don't get me wrong. I'm not a health-food sergeant. In fact, as I write this, there's a recipe for a flourless chocolate cake sitting on the kitchen counter, waiting to be born. What I am trying to say is that if you are going to cook with your kids, it'll do wonders for their palates if you try to prepare a wide variety of dishes, not just sweet ones.

## The Joy of Cooking . . . with Your Kids!

Before you imagine ingredients all over the floor and maybe even on the walls, take a deep breath, because it only takes a little bit of attention for you to spend quality time with your children that's fun and productive—not disastrous. Here are four great reasons to invite your children into the kitchen:

**1.** Cooking with your children helps them have a good attitude about food, even if they choose not to eat it. You are setting a great example for tasting new foods, and eventually they will catch on.

**2.** When kids participate in the creation of food that will be shared with the whole family, their self-esteem and confidence will soar! It shows you respect them and their abilities!

**3.** Cooking together builds social skills through sharing and cooperation.

**4.** Cooking together is also a great way for children to express their creativity, as they play with their food.

# RECIPE FOR COOKING WITH TODDLERS

**Ingredients:**

- ☐ 1 gallon patience
- ☐ 1 pinch expectations
- ☐ Several squirts of hand soap
- ☐ 2 dozen kitchen towels or rags (and maybe a mop)
- ☐ 1 set measuring cups
- ☐ 1 set measuring spoons

- ☐ 1 wooden spoon or silicone spatula
- ☐ Some inexpensive ingredients, such as water, dry rice, beans, or oatmeal (or try something that is safe for your dog to lick from the floor, such as flour, sugar, sunflower seeds, or dry cereal without raisins)
- ☐ 1 large mixing bowl with a nonskid bottom

**A few suggestions:**

If you woke up on the wrong side of the bed today, reconsider this activity. Have a glass of wine and get a good night's sleep—and try again tomorrow.

If you are new to cooking with your toddler, start by practicing a few techniques before preparing real food.

Read through the entire recipe and set up all of your tools and ingredients in advance, so that your young chef's attention span doesn't expire while waiting for you to get ready.

To prevent spills, pour ingredients over nested bowls. That way, if your young chef misses his target, the ingredients are still contained (and not all over your kitchen!).

If you don't have a mixing bowl with a nonskid bottom, put a damp dishcloth under the bowl. This will help to prevent it from sliding off the counter if your over-eager chef stirs a little too hard.

**Here's how to do it:**

Get excited and tell your toddler that you are going to play in the kitchen together. Pretending is the perfect way to start. Ask your toddler to look at the ingredients and name what you will be making together. Maybe it's oatmeal soup or a rice and bean jumble.

Bring a stool or chair into the kitchen, so your little chef can easily reach the sink to wash his hands.

Wash hands with soap and warm water. Don't forget to scritch and scratch the palm of each hand with the fingernails of the other. You never know what might be lurking under those nails.

Move the stool to the working area (such as the counter or the kitchen table).

Use the measuring spoons and measuring cups to measure quantities of whichever ingredients you have selected and pour them into a (nested) bowl.

Be sure to try using a variety of tools to stir these ingredients together (whisks, wooden spoons, spatulas, and even clean hands).

Toddlers need to get the feel of how hard to stir. Know ahead of time that some of your "soup" will slosh out over the sides of the bowl. That's okay!

Keep your eyes open for any nose picking, ear scratching, or tooth touching and use a happy voice as you bring your little chef back to the sink to wash her hands again.

Once you feel like your youngster has the hang of following directions and aiming ingredients over the mixing bowls, you are ready to move on to some "real" recipes!

## Using Recipes in This Book with Your Kids

Parenting would be way too easy if you knew exactly what to expect each step of the way. Luckily, kids keep you on your toes by developing at their own pace. You can make some generalizations, of course. Although some children are mature beyond their years, most toddlers have a short attention span and need to practice their fine motor skills. Older children are more coordinated and can follow a series of instructions instead of simply one step at a time. As their food preferences emerge, cooking together is more important than ever. As the kids interact with the food, the exposure they have to different ingredients will help them to taste and enjoy a wider variety of foods.

The seasonally inspired recipes in this book were selected because they are full of delicious, locally sourced, and nutritious foods—and because they are a blast to create with your children! Whether you have toddlers or preteens, there are recipes they can all help prepare. Of course, older kids can help out with steps designated as good ones for younger kids, but it shouldn't work in the other direction! The following color key shows how recipe steps are broken down by age appropriateness:

| 2–3 | 4–6 | 7–10 | 11+ |

2–3 = Blue        7–10 = Red
4–6 = Orange      11+  = Purple

## The Ultimate Timesavers

What? You don't have extra hours every day to spend in the kitchen? C'mon, it's not like you are busy working, folding laundry, walking the dog, shuttling to play dates and soccer games, or networking online. . . . Despite a harried schedule, it actually *is* possible to serve healthy food to your family, especially if you use these tips to help speed the process:

- **Plan Ahead.** Select all of the recipes that you plan to use for the week, so you don't have to shop at the last minute or resort to takeout. If you make a list for the week, you can shop for most of your ingredients in one trip.

- **Involve Your Kids.** While you are working on preparing dinner, put your dirty tools and dishes into a large bowl filled with soapy water in the sink. Kids love to get their hands wet, and can scrub the tools as you add them. You will be surprised at how well they can do the job, and how it will save you the time instead of doing the whole job yourself. Kids can also help you with prep work, menu planning, and grocery shopping.

- **Create One-Pot Meals.** These can save you time during meal preparation. Instead of cooking separate recipes for your protein, carbohydrates, and vegetables, try making one of the recipes in this book that includes all of these components, such Acorn Squash and Wild Rice Bowls or Wish-for-a-Fish Pasta.

- **Use a Slow Cooker.** Relying on this amazing appliance is a fantastic way to prepare a family meal with little fuss. Simply take a few minutes to prepare some ingredients the night before. In the morning, toss them into the slow cooker and the meal will be ready in time for dinner. I have been known to forget to get the ingredients into the slow cooker before leaving the house, so I put it on the counter the night before so that it jogs my memory in the morning.

- **Simplify.** Instead of preparing a salad, simply serve slices of vegetables and fruits as a side dish. Better yet, cut a few extra and store them in the refrigerator for a future meal or snack.

- **Make Extra Food.** If your recipe calls for two chicken breasts, make four instead. Use the leftovers in salads, quesadillas, or soups.

- **Stock Your Pantry.** Easy-to-use foods, such as canned beans, tomatoes, broth, salsa, marinara sauce, olives, and pasta can be a quick and healthy way to add flavor to your meals without making an extra trip to the market.

## Being Sneaky . . .

Many parents are plagued with power struggles at mealtimes. Children often protest about eating their vegetables or anything else that doesn't look familiar. And many parents, worried that their children will suffer from malnutrition, resort to puréeing vegetables and hiding them inside macaroni and cheese or brownies. Yep—for better or worse, it works. There may be fewer power struggles. The parents, knowing that dinner is spiked with hidden vegetables, encourage their children as they gobble up their favorite foods. The problem is that if children are unaware of the hidden ingredients in these recipes, they will continue to think of macaroni and cheese and brownies as healthy options—which they just might be at their own house, but elsewhere they may be overly processed and filled with inferior ingredients.

As a teacher of healthy cooking classes for kids, this concept has me torn. I love that kids are eating better, but they aren't eating better because they want to—they are eating well because they are being duped. When it comes to food, I feel that the most productive long-term tactic is to be honest with your children, so they can learn to make good choices for themselves and understand the benefits of eating well, both to their own health and the health of the planet.

## The Dessert Dilemma

Does this sound familiar: "How much more do I have to eat before I can have dessert?" If so, you're not alone. In fact, we started hearing this so often at our table that we decided to stop serving dessert every night. Dessert was becoming such a powerful incentive to eat their growing food that our kids were no longer listening to their bodies. Instead of considering how full they were, they were completely focused on the prize at the end. Now, we only offer dessert randomly, as an unexpected treat or as part of an afterschool snack. The pressure is off because dessert is no longer associated with their performance at the dinner table.

Consider this when entering into Dessert Negotiations with your children. By bargaining with your child about how much broccoli they have to eat before they get dessert, your child learns that dessert is better than broccoli. Otherwise, why would they have to bargain? Instead, if you want to include dessert every night, consider offering it with the meal. Some kids will eat dessert first, of course, but then they will most likely move on to the rest of their dinner.

As the parent, you're in the driver's seat when it comes to dessert. If you decide you would like to serve dessert, have options available that you feel good about serving your kids. Consider foods that are made from real ingredients, such as the Coconut Macaroons or Peaches and Cream Cobbler recipes you'll find later in the book, and not desserts with chemical names you can't pronounce.

Putting forth this kind of effort educating your children and cooking with them pays off in the most rewarding way as they become excited to try new foods and develop good eating habits that last a lifetime. By using fresh, seasonal, and local ingredients, children learn to appreciate color and crunch, and can be proud that they are eating foods that leave a smaller environmental footprint. What more could a caring parent ask for?

# Chapter 2
# Breakfast of Champions

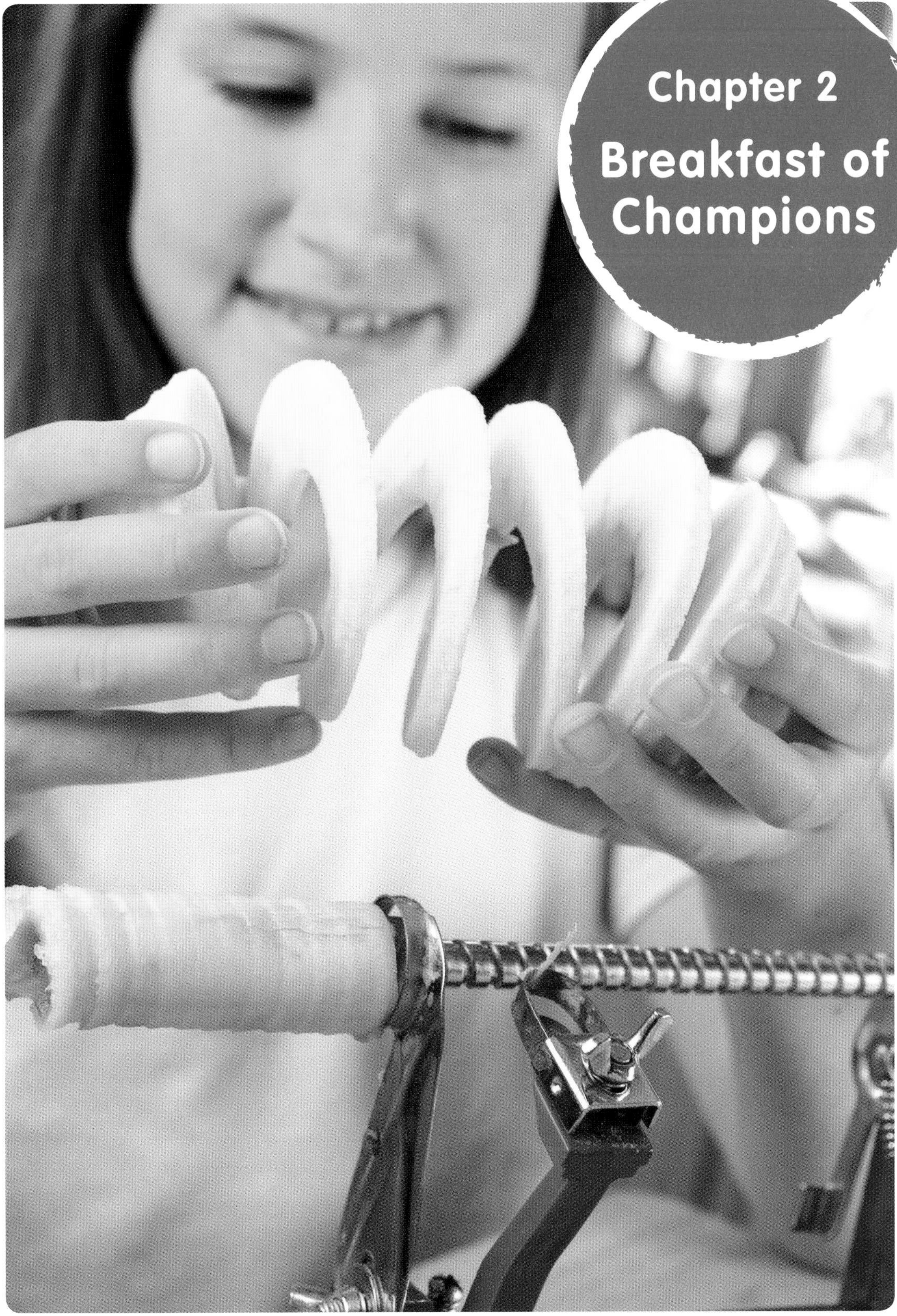

# Mini Frittatas

**Serves 4-6**

If you find yourself in a food rut, these mini frittatas may be your silver bullet! They are easy to prepare and make for a nutrient-packed breakfast. Plus, they store well and make a welcome change from PB&J in the lunch box!

☐ ⅓ cup freshly grated Parmesan, Asiago, or jack cheese

☐ 2 tablespoons chopped fresh Italian parsley leaves

☐ Optional additions: chopped turkey or ham, shredded potato, rosemary, or chopped veggies such as zucchini, mushrooms, spinach, or green onions

☐ Salt and pepper to taste

☐ 8 large eggs

☐ ¼ cup milk

| 2-3 | 4-6 | 7-10 | 11+ |
|---|---|---|---|

▶ Preheat oven to 375°F.

▶ Grate the cheese.

▶ Pick the parsley leaves from the stem and tear or cut them into small pieces. Save the stems for your chickens or the compost bin.

▶ Using a knife or a pair of kitchen scissors, cut the turkey, ham, or any veggies that you might be using.

▶ Mix together the grated cheese and chopped veggies and meat, if using.

▶ Season with salt and pepper.

▶ Spray the muffin tins with nonstick cooking spray.

▶ Using a teaspoon or small scoop, fill the 24 mini-muffin cups halfway with the cheese mixture.

▶ Crack the eggs over a small bowl. Fish out any stray shells before lightly beating them with a fork or whisk. Measure and add milk to the eggs. Use a ¼ cup measuring cup to pour the beaten eggs into the wells of the muffin pan.

▶ Bake until golden, about 12 minutes. Remove from the oven and let cool before removing from the pan.

▶ Store refrigerated in an airtight container and reheat for breakfast before school.

# Breakfast Anytime Pizza

**Serves 4-6**

I don't know about your family, but my kids and I love to eat leftover pizza for breakfast. This recipe puts a twist on the breakfast-for-dinner phenomenon that families adore. We're teaching the kids how to customize what would traditionally be a dinner recipe, and serving it for breakfast! Being flexible is a life skill, and this recipe gives kids firsthand experience at being adaptable. Be sure to let your little chef help you pick which of the toppings to use.

- ☐ 3 large russet potatoes
- ☐ 8 eggs
- ☐ 1 teaspoon kosher salt
- ☐ ¼ teaspoon black pepper
- ☐ ½ cup low-fat milk
- ☐ 1 clove garlic
- ☐ Freshly snipped herbs, to taste
- ☐ 6 mushrooms, sliced

- ☐ ½ can pitted black olives, sliced
- ☐ ½ red onion, sliced very thin
- ☐ ½ red bell pepper
- ☐ 2 Roma tomatoes, organic if possible
- ☐ 4 ounces Cheddar cheese, shredded
- ☐ 1 cup chopped ham, optional
- ☐ Salt and black pepper to taste

| 2-3 | 4-6 | **7-10** | **11+** |

**Prepare the shredded potato crust:**

▶ Preheat oven to 400°F.

▶ Wash potatoes, and shred them in a food processor.

▶ Transfer shredded potatoes to a large bowl.

▶ Set the kettle of water to high heat and once boiling, cover potatoes with the water and allow to set for 2 minutes.

▶ Drain the potatoes in a colander and press out as much water as you can. Pour the shredded potatoes onto a large, clean dish towel, and wrap the towel around them, lengthwise. Twist the ends of the towel, so that the bundle looks like a wrapped piece of saltwater taffy.

*continued on next page*

# Breakfast Anytime Pizza—continued

▶ Work with a partner to twist the ends of the towel over the sink, so that the potatoes get squeezed and the water squishes out. When you have squeezed out as much water as you can, pour the potatoes back into the large bowl.

▶ Crack one egg over a small bowl. Fish out any pieces of stray shell.

▶ Using a fork or a whisk, beat the egg lightly. Pour the egg into the potatoes.

▶ Add kosher salt and pepper.

▶ Mix together with clean hands.

▶ Spray a pizza stone or baking sheet with nonstick cooking spray.

▶ Use your hands to press the potato/egg mixture onto the stone (in whatever shape that works best). It should be no more than ½" thick.

▶ Bake crust at 400°F for 35 minutes or until golden brown.

▶ Meanwhile, crack the remaining eggs over a large bowl. Fish out any stray shells. Measure milk and add to eggs. Whisk them together.

▶ Peel the paper skin from the garlic. Press with a garlic press.

▶ Add the crushed garlic to the eggs.

▶ If desired, snip some fresh herbs, such as dill or thyme, and add them to the eggs before cooking them.

▶ Scramble the eggs in a skillet over medium heat. Remove and fluff cooked eggs with a fork.

**Prepare the pizza toppings:**

▶ Slice the mushrooms and olives. You can use a knife or an egg slicer.

▶ Using a very sharp knife cut the onion down the center vertically, from the stem to the tip. Place the onion, flat side down, on a cutting board and hold the end with your fingers tucked under and your fingernails pointing into the onion. Make thin slices across the onion.

▶ Chop the bell pepper into pieces approximately ¼–½" long. Thinly slice the tomatoes.

▶ Grate the cheese with a rotary or box grater.

**Build the pizza:**

▶ Spread the scrambled eggs onto the prebaked shredded potato crust.

▶ Sprinkle with salt and pepper, to taste.

▶ Spread the veggie toppings and cheese on top of the egg mixture.

▶ Bake for 10–15 minutes, or until the cheese has melted and the veggies have softened.

▶ Slice into wedges and serve while it is still hot.

## GOING GREEN
### Keeping Your Moo-lah Local

Ask around and I bet that you'll discover a dairy near your community that makes its own cheese. Different parts of the country produce cheeses that have their own local flavors. Just as a wine connoisseur can detect that grapes have been grown in different locations, cheese experts can identify subtle variations in flavor by region! Money spent locally on artisan products and ingredients travels through fewer hands, which means that more of the profit goes to the hands that feed you. Literally.

# Yummy Strawberry Yogurt Parfait

**Serves 4**

There is something extra special about this recipe. Maybe it's the fancy glass that we like to serve it in, but I suspect it is really the creaminess of the Greek-style yogurt. If you can't find this variety of yogurt at the store, here's a trick to try at home: Simply line a mesh strainer with a clean dishcloth or paper towels and pour in 2 cups of plain low-fat yogurt. Set the strainer over a bowl, cover with foil, and refrigerate overnight. The whey will drain out, leaving pure heaven behind.

- ☐ 2 cups granola
- ☐ 2 cups 2% Greek-style plain yogurt
- ☐ 1 cup strawberries, preferably organic
- ☐ 4 teaspoons honey

**2-3  4-6  7-10  11+**

▶ Measure granola and pour it into a bowl (you can use the Crunchy Granola recipe found later in the chapter, or you can use store-bought granola). Measure the yogurt and pour it into a bowl.

▶ Wash the strawberries.

▶ Cut off the stems, and slice the berries with an egg slicer or with a knife. Put them in a small bowl.

▶ Set out 4 fancy (but sturdy) glasses.

▶ In each glass, layer ¼ cup plain yogurt, ½ teaspoon honey, ¼ cup granola, and a small handful of berries. Repeat the layers one more time.

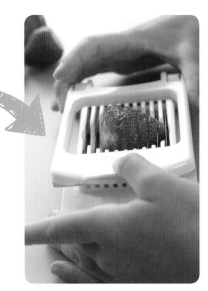

# Banana Sunshine Smoothie

 **Makes 1** Instead of tossing bananas that are past their prime, peel them and store them in a container in your freezer. Frozen bananas are an excellent addition to smoothies, and give a luscious sweet flavor and creamy texture to a summertime treat. That way, you can reduce, reuse, and recycle, right in your kitchen!

- ☐ 1 frozen banana
- ☐ ½ cup frozen strawberries and peaches
- ☐ ½ cup plain low-fat yogurt (try Greek yogurt; it's great!)
- ☐ ¾ cup orange juice

**2-3**　4-6　**7-10**　**11+**

▶ Break the frozen banana into 3 or 4 pieces and put the banana into the blender.

▶ Measure the frozen strawberries and peaches, yogurt, and juice and add them to the blender.

▶ Put on the lid, double checking to make sure that it is on tightly. Turn on the blender and blend until smooth.

# Sweet and Salty Glazed Bacon

 **Serves 6**

Bacon isn't the most common recipe to find in a book in which parents are encouraged to cook with their children. It's hot and it splatters—not a good combination for creating good memories in the kitchen with your family. But you'll love this method. It's safer, neater, and more kid-friendly. It is also less greasy because the bacon drains as it cooks and leaves the crispy meat behind.

- ☐ ⅓ cup lightly packed light-brown sugar
- ☐ 16 slices bacon (about 1 pound), free from nitrites and other preservatives, or from a local farm

**2-3**  **4-6**  **7-10**  **11+**

- ▶ Preheat oven to 350°F.

- ▶ Line two 10" x 15" rimmed baking sheets with foil. Place a wire cooling rack on top of each sheet.

- ▶ Measure the brown sugar and pour onto a dinner plate.

- ▶ Press one side of each bacon slice gently into the brown sugar.

- ▶ Arrange the bacon strips in a single layer on top of the racks. Be sure to wash little hands afterward.

- ▶ Bake for 30–35 minutes, rotating the sheets halfway through.

- ▶ The finished bacon should be crisp and browned. Serve alongside Mini Frittatas or Baked Apple Puff for a satisfying breakfast!

# Corny Raspberry Muffins

**Serves 12**

It can be crazy around our house in the morning—people are rushing in every direction, getting dressed, packing backpacks for school, and eating breakfast. Having healthy muffins on hand is really nice when time is short and you all need to grab something that is fast and easy to eat. These are better for you—and the planet—than the drive-through, any day!

- ☐ 1½ cups all-purpose flour
- ☐ ½ cup yellow cornmeal
- ☐ ½ cup packed brown sugar
- ☐ 1 teaspoon baking powder
- ☐ 1 teaspoon baking soda
- ☐ ¼ teaspoon salt

- ☐ 1¼ cups plain low-fat yogurt
- ☐ 3 tablespoons canola oil
- ☐ 1 lemon
- ☐ 2 large eggs, lightly beaten
- ☐ 1 cup fresh raspberries
- ☐ ½ teaspoon granulated sugar

| 2-3 | 4-6 | 7-10 | 11+ |

▶ Preheat oven to 375°F.

▶ Measure flour, cornmeal, brown sugar, baking powder, baking soda, and salt into a large bowl. In a separate bowl, mix yogurt and canola oil.

▶ Use a lemon zester, microplane, or box grater to grate the lemon rind over the bowl of dry ingredients. Watch out—these are sharp!

▶ Crack the eggs and add them to a separate small bowl.

▶ Lightly mix the eggs with a whisk or fork. Add the eggs to the yogurt mixture and stir to combine.

- ▶ Pour the wet mixture into the large bowl of dry ingredients.

- ▶ Stir until just blended. The dough won't be nice and tender if you overmix.

- ▶ Use a ¼ cup measuring cup to spoon the batter into the muffin tin (coated with nonstick spray).

- ▶ Mix the raspberries and sugar in a small bowl.

- ▶ Using a spoon, scoop even quantities of berries into each muffin cup.

- ▶ Bake for 20 minutes or until the muffins spring back when you touch them gently in the center. Remove them from the oven and let cool for 5 minutes in the pan.

- ▶ Remove the muffins from the pan and allow to cool on a wire rack before digging in!

## GOING GREEN
### Eating Local
# Tastes Better!

Consider buying your berries from your farmer's market. Local food doesn't have to travel very far, which means you will be able to eat it at the peak of its ripeness. Not only will it taste better, it'll be more nutrient-dense! Another benefit to supporting the local growers? You send a message to the producers who transport food via planes, boats, trains, and trucks, all with high carbon dioxide emissions that are lousy for our air quality. If you don't buy it, maybe they won't ship it!

# Baked Apple Puff

**Serves 4**

We love adaptable recipes, especially ones that taste great any time of the day. My kids love eating breakfast for dinner, and I have to admit that I adore it too. It's hard to resist serving this Baked Apple Puff, since it's built from protein and fruit. It is also the ideal locavore dish for our family. Our daughter is in 4-H and we have a small flock of chickens in the back yard. We also have a small apple tree. Between the two, the ingredients for this dish couldn't come from a source any closer!

- ☐ 5 tablespoons butter, divided
- ☐ 3 eggs
- ☐ ¾ cup milk
- ☐ 3 tablespoons granulated sugar, divided
- ☐ ½ teaspoon pure vanilla extract
- ☐ 1¼ teaspoons ground cinnamon, divided
- ☐ ¼ teaspoon salt
- ☐ ½ cup flour
- ☐ 2 small crisp apples, organic if possible (go for Fuji if you prefer a slightly sweet apple, or Granny Smith if you enjoy a tart flavor)

| 2-3 | 4-6 | 7-10 | 11+ |

▶ Preheat oven to 450°F.

▶ Melt 2 tablespoons of butter in the microwave or in a saucepan.

▶ In a medium-sized bowl, crack the eggs.

▶ Beat the eggs lightly and then add the melted butter.

▶ Measure milk, 1 tablespoon sugar, vanilla, ¼ teaspoon ground cinnamon, salt, and flour, and add them to the eggs.

- ▶ Mix all of the ingredients until the batter is well blended.

- ▶ If you have one, use an apple peeler/corer/slicer to peel, core, and slice your apples. If not, use a vegetable peeler to peel the apples.

- ▶ Cut out the cores and slice the apples thinly.

- ▶ Heat the remaining 3 tablespoons butter in a 10" ovenproof skillet. Add the sliced apples and cook until they are golden brown, 5–10 minutes. (If you'd like, you can add a dash or two of ground cinnamon.)

- ▶ Put on oven mitts and take the skillet off the heat. Pour the batter over the apples.

- ▶ Measure 2 tablespoons granulated sugar and 1 teaspoon cinnamon and stir them together in a small bowl. Sprinkle the cinnamon sugar over the batter.

- ▶ Place the skillet into the oven and cook for 15–25 minutes until gently browned and puffed. (Do not open the oven during the first 15 minutes of the cooking process, or the puff will deflate!)

- ▶ Put on oven mitts, remove the skillet from the oven, and immediately place an oven mitt over the handle, so that you won't accidentally burn your hand.

- ▶ Cut the puff into wedges and serve immediately.

# Steel-Cut Oatmeal with Dates

**Serves 4**

This recipe uses steel-cut oats, which many cooks are not familiar with. When you buy oats there are three main types you can choose from. The most common are old-fashioned rolled oats, which have been rolled flat and steamed. Quick oats are also common, and are essentially rolled oats that have been ground up into smaller pieces so they cook a little bit faster. Then there are steel-cut oats. These are formed when the inside of the raw oat is sliced by a blade into several small pieces. They look like grains of brown rice, taste slightly nutty, and have a firmer texture than their rolled cousins, which tend to be mushy when cooked. Steel-cut oats take longer to prepare than old-fashioned or quick oats, but after tasting this sweet, winter-warming recipe, you'll find it's worth the wait!

- ☐ 1 cup steel-cut oats
- ☐ 3 cups boiling water
- ☐ 1 cup low-fat milk (soy milk, rice milk, or coconut milk are great alternatives)
- ☐ ¼ teaspoon salt
- ☐ 1 cup diced fresh dates (about 8 dates)
- ☐ 3 tablespoons butter
- ☐ ⅛ teaspoon salt
- ☐ ¼ teaspoon ground cinnamon
- ☐ 1 teaspoon honey
- ☐ ½ teaspoon vanilla

**Cook the oatmeal:**

▶ Measure the steel-cut oats and pour them into a large saucepot.

▶ Turn on the heat to medium-high, and heat the oats gently until they become fragrant, about 2 minutes.

▶ Boil water and add to the oats.

▶ Reduce the heat and simmer the oats for 20 minutes.

▶ Measure the milk and add it to the cooking oatmeal. Stir to combine and cook for an additional 10 minutes.

**Prepare the date topping:**

▶ While the oatmeal is cooking, cut the dates into small pieces, making sure to remove the pits.

▶ In a small skillet, melt the butter over medium heat. Add the diced dates and stir to combine.

▶ Measure the salt, cinnamon, honey, and vanilla, and add to the cooking dates. Stir to combine. Reduce the heat to low and allow the flavors to combine for 3 minutes.

**Assemble:**

▶ Spoon the oatmeal into 4 bowls and top with the sweet date mixture.

▶ The dates will be very hot, so be sure that your kids allow them to cool down a little before digging in!

# Sweet Potato Biscuits

*Recipe adapted with permission from Janisse Scott of Family Bites.*

**Serves many!** These warm and flaky biscuits will give your kids a reason to haul themselves out of bed before school. If you have any left, store them in an airtight container and heat them gently in the toaster oven before serving. Even though sweet potatoes are unrelated to the potato, both grow underground and can be found with a variety of skin colors. See if you can find ones with white, red, purple, and golden skin at your farmer's market, and have a taste test with your kids. This will serve a hungry family of 4 for a few days!

- ☐ 1 large sweet potato
- ☐ Pinch of salt
- ☐ 1¼ cups unbleached all-purpose flour
- ☐ ½ cup whole wheat flour
- ☐ 1 tablespoon dark brown sugar
- ☐ 2½ teaspoons baking powder
- ☐ ½ teaspoon baking soda
- ☐ ¼ teaspoon cayenne pepper, optional
- ☐ ½ cup butter, chilled
- ☐ ⅓ cup buttermilk, chilled

**2-3**  4-6  **7-10**  **11+**

▶ Preheat the oven to 425°F.

▶ Line a baking sheet with a Silpat (a reusable nonstick silicone mat) or unbleached parchment paper.

▶ Peel the sweet potato with a vegetable peeler.

▶ Cut it in half, and place the flat side on the cutting board so that it doesn't wobble.

▶ Cut the sweet potato into ½" cubes.

▶ Put cubes into a saucepan, cover with water, and add a pinch of salt. Bring the water to a boil and cook for 6–8 minutes or until they are easily pierced with a fork.

▶ Drain the water in a colander in the sink and return the potatoes to the pan.

▶ Using a potato masher, mash the potatoes.

▶ Measure the flours, sugar, baking powder, baking soda, and cayenne, if using. Add them to a medium-sized mixing bowl and whisk to combine.

▶ Remove the butter from the refrigerator and cut into ½" cubes.

▶ Add the butter to the flour mixture and rub together with your hands or mix with a pastry blender until it the texture is crumbly. You could also pulse the mixture together in a food processor.

▶ Measure the buttermilk and mashed sweet potatoes (about ½–¾ cup) and stir them in a bowl until they are smooth.

▶ Add the flour mixture and knead with clean hands inside the bowl until the dough comes together.

▶ Sprinkle some flour on a clean work surface (a large cutting board or the counter). Place the dough onto the floured surface and pat into a 1"-thick circle.

▶ Use a round cookie cutter (any size is fine, but 2" wide is ideal) to cut out biscuits. Place the biscuits on the prepared baking sheet.

▶ Bake for 8–10 minutes or until tops are golden brown. Remove from oven and cool slightly before eating. These are delish with scrambled eggs or a bowl of yogurt and fruit!

# Breakfast Burrito

**Serves 4**

When our hectic schedules allow it, we eat as a family around the kitchen table. But sometimes we have to eat on the run. Instead of taking our food in the car inside disposable plastic bags or foil, we try to opt for foods that can be eaten over a plate or a reusable container with a lid. One of the perks of these delicious breakfast burritos is that they come inside their own wrapper! If your little ones are a little clumsy, like one of mine, be sure to take this on the road on a plate in case some of the beans decide to jump ship.

□ 1 russet potato

□ 2 teaspoons canola oil

□ 2 chicken apple sausages (you can also use spicy sausage or chorizo)

□ 4 eggs

□ ¼ teaspoon cumin

□ 1 cup cooked or canned black beans

□ Salt and freshly ground black pepper

□ ⅓ cup Cheddar, feta, or queso fresco cheese

□ 4 10" whole wheat tortillas

□ ¼ cup sour cream

□ ¼ cup salsa

□ 1 handful fresh cilantro or parsley leaves, optional

□ 1 small avocado, optional

□ 2 slices cooked bacon or turkey bacon, crumbled, optional

□ Hot sauce, optional

**2-3**  4-6  **7-10**  **11+**

▶ Scrub the potato under running water.

▶ Prick it all over with a fork and cook it in the microwave for 5–6 minutes, or until tender. Or bake at 350°F for up to an hour, until easily pierced with a knife. Allow it to cool while you prepare the other ingredients.

▶ Heat the canola oil in a skillet over a medium-high heat.

*continued*

## Breakfast Burrito—continued

▶ Slice the sausages into ¼"-thick rounds. (Note: If you are using uncooked sausages, you will need to squeeze it from its casing.)

▶ Cook the sausage in the skillet until it is browned.

▶ Crack the eggs into a medium-sized bowl. Beat with a fork or whisk. Measure the cumin and add it to the eggs.

▶ Reduce the heat to medium-low and pour the eggs into the skillet with the sausage. Stir them occasionally and break up any large clumps.

▶ Meanwhile, cut the baked potato into 1" cubes and set aside.

▶ Drain and rinse the black beans and add them to the skillet so that they can warm through.

▶ Season the egg, sausage, and bean mixture with salt and pepper to taste and remove the skillet from the heat.

▶ Grate or crumble the cheese into a small dish.

▶ Spread each tortilla with sour cream and salsa, if desired.

▶ Put ¼ of the potato cubes onto the center of each tortilla. Top the potato with ¼ of the egg, sausage, and bean mixture.

▶ Sprinkle with cheese.

▶ Add any additional toppings you like, such as cilantro, diced avocado, crumbled bacon, or hot sauce.

▶ To roll your burrito, bring one side toward the center, covering the toppings. Then do the same with the bottom, the second side, and then the top.

▶ Eat whole or cut the burrito in half, for little hands.

# ☑ RECIPE FOR ACTION
## Cook for Others!

There are lots of ways that children and their families can use food to help the hungry people in their community. While some activities take lots of planning and volunteers, here is a simple idea you can pull off with the help of a few friends.

**1.** Simply get together and make a grocery list for your favorite burrito recipe. Based on your budget, decide how many burritos you want to make—and be sure that you get enough ingredients.

**2.** Go to the grocery store and get your ingredients and supplies. To keep costs down, buy dried beans and cook them yourself.

**3.** Prepare your ingredients. If you are cooking dried beans, you will need to soak them overnight.

**4.** Make your burritos, wrap them in foil, and keep them warm in the oven.

**5.** Pack them in backpacks and ride your bikes around town, delivering them to people who seem hungry. If it isn't safe to ride bicycles in your town, perhaps you and your kids can drive to a park or soup kitchen where hungry people might gather.

**6.** Hand them out with a smile—your kids will feel proud that they helped someone today!

# Grilled Cheese with Nutella

**Makes 4**

You have heard the expression a million times. Breakfast is the most important meal of the day. Since many families struggle to wake kids up on time, navigate piles of laundry, and locate misplaced shoes, it can be hard to find the time for breakfast. Using this recipe as an occasional lure, your kids are sure to get ready for school in a jiffy. Even though this breakfast is sweeter than we usually eat, the rich and delicious flavor will motivate them to hurry up and see what is on the breakfast table the next time.

- ☐ 3 tablespoons unsalted butter, softened
- ☐ 8 slices rustic white bread (¼"-thick slices)
- ☐ ¼ cup chocolate hazelnut spread, such as Nutella, at room temperature
- ☐ 1 cup ricotta cheese, at room temperature

`2-3`  `4-6`  `7-10`  `11+`

▶ Spread butter on one side of each slice of bread. Place the buttered side down on a clean work surface.

▶ Spread Nutella and ricotta on 4 slices of bread, and top with the remaining slices, buttered side up.

▶ Place a large skillet over low heat. (By cooking the sandwiches on low, you won't burn the bread but the sandwiches will get warm enough for the cheese to melt.)

*continued on next page*

## Grilled Cheese with Nutella—continued

▶ Place 2 sandwiches at a time in the skillet. Press down on the sandwiches with the back of a spatula, so that they sizzle.

▶ Cook for at least 5 minutes, or until the undersides begin to turn golden brown.

▶ Flip the sandwiches and cook for 5 minutes more, until the bottoms are browned to your liking. Cool slightly and gobble up!

# Crunchy Granola

**Makes 5 cups\*** Each time I shop, I gaze at the shelves and consider the prices of packages in front of me. How much of that fee goes toward the bag? The box? The actual food inside? You couldn't ask for an easier recipe to prepare yourself than granola. And the cost can't be beat. Plus, there is no unnecessary packaging—simply store it in an airtight container. The only hazard is that it might disappear quickly!

- ☐ 4 cups oats (not quick-cooking)
- ☐ ⅓ cup brown sugar
- ☐ 3 tablespoons sesame seeds
- ☐ ½ teaspoon salt
- ☐ 1 teaspoon cinnamon
- ☐ ¼ cup honey
- ☐ ¼ cup canola oil
- ☐ 2 teaspoons vanilla extract

**\*Optional Ingredients (will increase the yield):**

- ☐ ¼ cup dried, shredded coconut
- ☐ ¼ cup sunflower seeds (without shells)
- ☐ ¼ cup pumpkin seeds
- ☐ 3 tablespoons flaxseed
- ☐ ½ cup nuts, chopped (almonds, walnuts, pecans, or cashews are all great!)
- ☐ ⅓ cup dried fruit, such as cranberries, raisins, currants, blueberries, or cherries

2-3  4-6  7-10  **11+**

▶ Preheat the oven to 300°F.

▶ Measure oats, brown sugar, sesame seeds, salt, and cinnamon, and combine them in a large bowl. If using, add shredded coconut, sunflower and/or pumpkin seeds, flaxseed, and nuts.

▶ Measure honey, oil, and vanilla, and combine them in a separate bowl. Pour honey mixture over the oat mixture and stir to combine.

▶ Pour the granola onto a greased rimmed baking sheet and spread into an even layer.

*continued on next page*

**Crunchy Granola—continued**

▶ Bake for 25–30 minutes, stirring gently every 10 minutes, so that the granola doesn't burn.

▶ After the granola comes out of the oven and cools, add any dried fruit of your choice.

▶ Once cooled, store in an airtight container for up to 10 days.

## GOING GREEN
## The Great Pacific Garbage Patch

Most of the time, when we hear about a new island, we picture palm trees, sandy beaches, and sunny blue skies. Sadly, the same can't be said for our natural reaction of disgust when scientists discovered the Great Pacific Garbage Patch. It is a floating island in the Pacific Ocean made from bits of plastics and garbage. Brought together by winds and ocean currents, the mass has grown to be the size of Texas. Why on earth would I mention this in a cookbook, or all places? There are two good reasons.

First, the trash, degraded by the sun and waves, is broken into tiny pieces that may resemble food and be consumed by marine life. Not only can this harm the animals that ingest these items, but it also disrupts the whole marine food chain, upon which we rely.

Second, as the people who are producing the trash, we are responsible. By taking simple steps, such as having a garden and making our own food from scratch, we can reduce the packaging we use and the garbage that we produce. The sea turtles and their friends will thank you.

Chapter 3
Lunchtime Favorites

# A-B-C Frittata

 **Serves 4-6** The A-B-C in this recipe stands for Apple-Bacon-Cheddar! When I was a child, I was obsessed with animals. I never dreamed that when I became an adult, my family would have a flock of chickens in the backyard! This is the perfect recipe to make use of our plethora of fresh eggs. Not only is it delicious warm, but it also packs well in an insulated bag for school lunches.

- ☐ 10 eggs
- ☐ 1 cup Cheddar cheese, grated
- ☐ Salt and ground pepper, to taste
- ☐ 3 slices bacon, cooked and crumbled
- ☐ 2 apples, Fuji or Gala
- ☐ 1 tablespoon butter

`2-3`  `4-6`  `7-10`  `11+`

▶ Put the oven rack in the upper third of the oven and preheat to 450°F.

▶ Crack 8 eggs, one at a time, and pour each egg into a medium bowl. Check for shells.

▶ You need only the whites from the remaining 2 eggs. To separate the egg whites, crack the egg over an egg separator or someone's clean hands. Carefully let the egg white slip through the fingers into the bowl, with the yolk remaining.

▶ Using a whisk, beat the eggs until the yolks and whites are thoroughly combined.

▶ Grate the cheese with a box grater. (Younger children can help you if they use a rotary cheese grater, which protects their knuckles.)

▶ Add half of the grated cheese to the egg mixture and stir to combine.

▶ Add a pinch of salt and pepper.

- Cook the strips of bacon. You can fry them in a skillet (watch out—they can splatter!) or you can bake them in a 425°F oven on a cooling rack placed on a rimmed baking sheet. This is a great method because you don't have to flip the bacon, and the kids stay safe.

- Once the bacon cools, crumble the strips with clean hands.

- Use an apple peeler/corer/slicer on the apple. If you don't have one, use a vegetable peeler to peel the apple.

- If you have an apple corer, you may use it. Or, simply cut up the apple, leaving the core behind.

- Slice the apple pieces very thinly. As you are cutting, make sure the apple pieces are flat-side down, so the chunks don't wobble on the cutting board.

- In a medium cast-iron or nonstick ovenproof skillet, heat the butter over medium heat.

- Add egg mixture to the skillet and sprinkle the bacon crumbles evenly over the eggs.

- Gently arrange the apple slices on top of the egg mixture, in a circular pattern, and sprinkle with remaining cheese.

- Move the skillet from the stovetop to the upper rack of your oven.

- Bake until frittata is firm in the center and cheese is browned, about 20 minutes.

- Put on an oven mitt and remove the skillet from the oven. Use a flexible spatula to loosen the frittata from the pan and carefully slide it onto a cutting board.

- Allow to cool for a few minutes before slicing into wedges and eating.

  *Note:* Egg yolks can be frozen for later recipes. Simply pour each yolk into the well of an ice cube tray. Sprinkle each yolk with a pinch of sugar or salt, depending on whether you plan to use them for sweet or savory dishes. Cover the tray and freeze.

## GOING GREEN
# Don't Be Chicken . . .

There is something to be said for being old-fashioned. When I think of the stories that our grandparents told us about growing up, there are many similarities, no matter where they came from. They gardened, "put up" summer produce in jars for the lean winters, and mended clothes, rather than replacing them. Maybe instead of thinking of these characteristics as old-fashioned, we should consider them ahead of their time. They were eco-conscious!

While having backyard chickens may seem like a new trend, all it takes is one look back into your family tree to see that it's not new at all. Chickens eat food scraps, bugs, and weeds and give you rich fertilizer at the same time. It seems they fit beautifully into the recycling mindset that has been around for generations. Before building a coop, check with your local government to see if your area allows residents to keep chickens!

# Wrap It Up: BBQ Style

**Serves many!*** Some kids enjoy finding the same items in their school lunch every day. But other kids want you to mix things up a bit. Here is a formula for making a delicious winter-warming wrap. You can use the same method for making a variety of other wraps as well. Be sure to talk to your kids about their favorite ingredients, so they are excited to see what you created. Or better yet, let them customize the wraps themselves.

*Makes as many wraps as you have ingredients for!*

- ☐ Cream cheese
- ☐ BBQ sauce
- ☐ Whole wheat flour tortillas
- ☐ Lettuce
- ☐ Carrots
- ☐ Cheddar cheese
- ☐ Roasted turkey or braised tofu (found in the refrigerated produce section of the grocery store, with the regular tofu)
- ☐ Crumbled bacon, optional

`2-3` `4-6` `7-10` `11+`

▶ Combine cream cheese and BBQ sauce, to taste.

▶ Spread the cream cheese mixture on each tortilla.

▶ Slice or tear the lettuce into strips.

▶ Grate the carrots and Cheddar cheese.

▶ Slice the roasted turkey. Or,

▶ Crumble the braised tofu.

▶ Layer the lettuce, carrots, Cheddar, and roasted turkey or braised tofu onto the tortilla.

▶ Top with a bit of crumbled bacon, if desired.

▶ Fold up the side farthest from you. Roll the tortilla from left to right and place it with the seam side down on your serving plate or in your reusable school lunch container.

# Squashed Sweet Potato Soup

**Serves 6**

Send your kids to school with a thermos of this soup for lunch, and when they eat it, they will feel like you just gave them a big warm hug. Smooth and hearty, this soup will give your children the energy they need to stay focused for the rest of the school day.

- ☐ 1 large butternut squash (or about 4 cups, puréed)
- ☐ 2 medium-sized sweet potatoes
- ☐ 2 tablespoons butter
- ☐ 2 or 3 fresh sage leaves
- ☐ 2 shallots
- ☐ 1 clove garlic
- ☐ 4 cups vegetable broth
- ☐ Salt and pepper to taste
- ☐ Apple cider vinegar, optional before serving

`2-3` `4-6` `7-10` `11+`

▶ Adults only for this step! Using a chef's knife or cleaver, cut the butternut squash in half.

▶ Scoop out the seeds with a spoon and set them aside for your compost or backyard chickens.

▶ Cook the squash until it is tender, at 375°F for about 45 minutes, cut side down with a little water poured onto a rimmed baking sheet. (Roasting the squash concentrates the flavor, making for a richer soup.)

▶ Meanwhile, use a vegetable peeler to peel the sweet potatoes.

*continued on next page*

# Squashed Sweet Potato Soup—continued

▶ Cut the sweet potatoes into cubes and steam them over 1 cup water, until tender, about 10–15 minutes. Alternatively, you can halve the sweet potatoes and roast them with the squash.

▶ In a stockpot, melt the butter over low heat. Add the sage leaves to pot so that their flavor gets infused into the melted butter.

▶ Mince the shallots and add them to the melted butter. Cook until they have softened, 3–5 minutes, stirring often. After the shallots have finished cooking, remove the sage leaves from the pot and discard. Turn off the heat under the pot.

▶ Peel the clove of garlic, press with a garlic press, and put it into the pot.

▶ Once cooked and cool enough to handle, scrape the softened butternut squash from the skin and add it to the stockpot. Also add the steamed or roasted sweet potatoes and turn the heat back on to medium.

▶ Measure the vegetable broth and add it to the pot.

▶ When all of the ingredients have heated through, stir to combine and reduce heat to low, and cook for 10 minutes.

▶ Blend the soup with an immersion blender (being careful it does not splash out of the pot) or by blending it in several small batches in a blender. (If you are using the blender, leave the cover slightly askew to allow the steam to escape.)

▶ Heat the soup for an additional 10 minutes and season with salt and pepper.

▶ Ladle the soup into individual bowls and add a small splash of apple cider vinegar to each, before serving, if desired. This soup also freezes very well, making it a great make-ahead staple when squash is in season!

# GOING GREEN

## Pay Dirt:
## Make Your Own
## Compost

Healthy gardens only grow from healthy soil. If your soil is old and anemic like ours was, you can amend it by making your own compost, which adds fertility and improves soil structure. Composting is recycling at its finest. Simply mix together a combination of the "ingredients" in the following list, make sure they stay moist, and turn the pile every so often. Nature will do its business and the ingredients will come together to create the cocktail of your garden's dreams.

**Do include:** plant materials, including a mixture of "browns" and "greens." Browns include dried leaves, wood chips or shavings, and seedless hay and straw (do you have a horse stable nearby?). Greens include weeds (without seed heads!), vegetable peels, fruit scraps, and grass clippings. You can also add coffee grounds as well as poop from rabbits, horses, goats, and chickens.

**Don't include:** any animal products (such as meat, bones, and dairy), diseased plants, or poop from carnivorous animals such as dogs or cats.

# Wrap It Up: L'egg-o Style

**Serves many!*** I surely can't be the only parent who occasionally has to scrape through the dregs of the refrigerator to make lunch for my children. Even though I am not always as well stocked as I would like to be, I always have tortillas and eggs on hand, which are the main ingredients in this simple recipe. And by keeping a small pot of lettuces on the deck, I have easy access to fresh greens any time my refrigerator runs dry. For their small size, they pack a significant nutritional punch, filled with protein, folate, iron, and zinc.

*Makes as many wraps as you have ingredients for!*

☐ Mayonnaise

☐ Whole wheat flour tortillas

☐ Romaine or butter lettuce

☐ Black olives

☐ Hard-boiled eggs

☐ Curry powder, optional

☐ Salt, to taste

| 2–3 | 4–6 | 7–10 | 11+ |
|-----|-----|------|-----|

▶ Spread a thin layer of mayonnaise on a tortilla.

▶ Slice or tear the lettuce into strips. Set aside.

▶ Use an egg slicer to slice the black olives. (If you prefer a finer consistency, you or an older child can chop them.)

▶ Mash the hard-boiled eggs with the back of a fork or with a potato masher.

▶ Mix in the black olives.

▶ Add a small dollop of mayonnaise and a touch of curry powder and salt, if desired.

▶ Stir to combine the flavors.

▶ Place some lettuce on the tortilla and top it with some egg salad.

▶ Fold up the side farthest from you. Roll the tortilla from left to right and place it with the seam side down on your serving plate or in your reusable school lunch container.

# Thai Spring Rolls

**Serves 4**

*Light*, *delicious*, and *filling* are just three words that come to mind when I think of this recipe. There are plenty of steps to keep all of the kids busy as they assemble these little beauties—and they are quick to gobble them up.

- ☐ 1–2 cups bean thread noodles
- ☐ 2 cloves garlic
- ☐ 1 teaspoon lime juice
- ☐ 1 tablespoon seasoned rice vinegar
- ☐ 2 teaspoons miso paste
- ☐ Smoked or braised tofu (available in the produce section of most grocery stores)
- ☐ 1 carrot
- ☐ 1 cup fresh bean sprouts
- ☐ 1 handful fresh basil or mint leaves
- ☐ 8 sheets of rice paper (spring roll wrappers)
- ☐ Sweet chili dipping sauce, optional

2-3 | 4-6 | 7-10 | 11+

**Prepare the noodles:**

▶ Soak bean thread noodles in boiling water until soft. Drain in a colander in the sink.

▶ Using clean scissors, snip the noodles into pieces about 1" long and put them into a large bowl.

▶ Peel the paper skin from the garlic.

*continued on next page*

## Thai Spring Rolls—continued

▶ Mash the garlic and put it into a bowl.

▶ Cut the lime in half.

▶ Squeeze the lime and measure 1 teaspoon of juice into the bowl with the garlic. Measure the rice vinegar and miso paste, and add them to the lime juice and garlic mixture and stir so all of the ingredients blend together. Pour the sauce over the noodles and combine well.

**Prepare the other fillings:**

▶ Open your package of tofu, and cut into thin slices. Since it is soft, a butter knife or plastic knife will work fine. Put the pieces of tofu on a plate and set aside until you are ready to fill your spring rolls.

▶ Use a vegetable peeler to cut thin slices of carrot. Or grate the carrot with either a rotary cheese grater or box grater. Set the grated carrot aside.

▶ Cut some basil or mint leaves into thin strips with clean scissors.

**Assemble the spring rolls:**

▶ Pour some warm water into a large bowl or a glass baking dish with sides.

▶ Dip a sheet of rice paper in warm water until it softens. Lay the softened rice paper wrapper on a clean surface, such as a plate or cutting board.

▶ Onto the wrapper, put a few pieces of tofu, a large pinch each of bean sprouts and shredded carrots, basil or mint leaves, and a large pinch of bean thread noodles.

▶ Gently wrap the rice paper, burrito-style. Fold one side toward the middle. Then fold up the bottom, then the other side, followed by the top. Be sure that it is wrapped tightly, enclosing the filling firmly. If the wrapper gets wrinkled or tears, you can simply wrap it in a second wrapper to neaten it up.

▶ Place on a plate with the seam underneath.

▶ If you prefer, slice each roll in half and serve with sweet chili dipping sauce.

# Smashed Avocado on Toast

**Serves 2**

Avocado is an ideal growing food, complete with vitamins and oils to help with brain development. You can scoop it right out of the peel and eat it with a spoon, you can mash it into guacamole, or you can spread it on toast for a light and healthy summertime lunch.

- ☐ 2 slices whole grain sandwich bread
- ☐ Olive oil
- ☐ Salt or Parmesan cheese, to taste
- ☐ 1 avocado
- ☐ ½ lemon or lime

| 2-3 | 4-6 | 7-10 | 11+ |

▶ Toast bread until light brown and crispy. Carefully remove from the toaster and put it on a plate.

▶ Pour 2–4 teaspoons of olive oil in a small bowl.

▶ Using a pastry brush, brush the olive oil onto one side of each slice of bread.

▶ Sprinkle the bread lightly with salt or Parmesan, your choice.

▶ Cut open the avocado and remove the pit.

▶ Scoop out the flesh with a spoon and put it on the toast. Using a butter knife, spread the avocado evenly on the toast.

▶ Squeeze the lemon or lime over the avocado and sprinkle again with a teensy bit of salt or Parmesan.

## KID ZONE
## Fruit or Vegetable?

Are avocados fruits or vegetables? They are commonly served in salads with other veggies like lettuce and carrots. But they are really fruits!

See if your friends think these items are fruits or veggies: tomatoes, squash, zucchini, cucumbers, bell peppers, chili peppers, pumpkins, green beans, and eggplant.

Surprise! Every one of them is a fruit. Fruits don't need to be sweet—they just need to contain seeds!

# Chinese Chicken Salad

**Serves 4**

Many farmer's markets have meat vendors who sell chicken raised humanely on local farms. If you cannot find a local source for your poultry, talk to the butcher in your neighborhood grocery store about which ones are raised free of hormones and antibiotics.

- ☐ 4 tablespoons soy sauce
- ☐ 2 teaspoons sesame oil
- ☐ 1 pound chicken breast, boneless and skinless
- ☐ ½ head green cabbage
- ☐ ¼ head red cabbage
- ☐ 1 large carrot
- ☐ 3 scallions, trimmed and thinly sliced, greens included (about ½ cup)
- ☐ 1 (11-ounce) can mandarin oranges in water
- ☐ 1 can sliced water chestnuts (8 ounces)
- ☐ 1 teaspoon salt
- ☐ ½ teaspoon ground pepper
- ☐ 2 tablespoons sugar (or 1 tablespoon agave nectar)
- ☐ 3 tablespoons canola oil
- ☐ 1 tablespoon sesame oil
- ☐ 4 tablespoons rice vinegar
- ☐ ¼ cup sliced almonds, toasted

`2-3` `4-6` `7-10` `11+`

▶ Preheat oven to 350°F.

▶ Measure soy sauce and sesame oil.

▶ Stir them together.

▶ Put the chicken in a baking dish (with sides). Using a pastry or basting brush, brush the soy sauce mixture onto the raw chicken.

▶ Cook the chicken until the juices run clear (15–30 minutes, depending on the size of the chicken pieces).

▶ Remove the chicken from the oven and allow to cool.

▶ Cut into thin slices.

▶ Slice the green and red cabbage into thin ribbons (slice into the whole head with a sharp knife).

▶ Put the cabbage into a large bowl.

▶ Grate the carrot with a rotary cheese grater or on the side of a box grater.

*continued on next page*

This salad can easily be made with tofu instead of chicken—the perfect adaptation if you would like to have a fresh and healthy meal for "Meatless Monday." Farm animals require lots of food and water, and of course they produce loads of methane, which causes global warming, and poop, which can pollute local waterways and groundwater. By going vegetarian at least one day of the week, you can reduce the environmental impact of the meat industry. We fondly call that "voting with your fork."

## Chinese Chicken Salad
## —continued

▶ Add the shredded carrots to the bowl.

▶ Using clean scissors, snip the scallions into small pieces (about ¼").

▶ Open the can of mandarin oranges and the can of sliced water chestnuts.

▶ Drain the oranges and water chestnuts in a colander over the sink, rinse them in fresh water, and add them to the bowl.

▶ Add the pieces of chicken to the bowl.

**To make the dressing:**

▶ Measure salt, pepper, sugar, canola and sesame oils, and rice vinegar and put in a bowl.

▶ Whisk together and pour dressing over the salad.

▶ Mix the salad together with clean hands or salad tongs and top with toasted almonds, if desired.

*Note:* You can also use leftover chicken for this recipe. Simply toss bite-sized pieces of cooked chicken with the soy sauce and sesame oil for flavor.

# There's Turkey in My Pocket

 **Serves 3–6\*** Aside from sharing a delicious meal with family, one of the best parts of Thanksgiving is the leftovers! Transform your leftover turkey into this light and whimsical salad filled with color, flavor, and crunch. Best of all, it's served in a pocket!

*\*Serving size depends on the size and appetite*

- ☐ 3 large lettuce leaves, romaine or butter
- ☐ 2 stalks celery
- ☐ ¼ cup dried cranberries
- ☐ ¼ cup dried plums (prunes), pitted and diced
- ☐ 2 tablespoons chives, optional
- ☐ 2 cups turkey, diced
- ☐ ½ cup plain low-fat yogurt
- ☐ Salt and pepper
- ☐ 3 whole wheat pita breads, halved

| 2-3 | 4-6 | 7-10 | 11+ |

▶ Wash lettuce leaves and dry with a clean towel.

▶ Rinse celery.

▶ Use a vegetable peeler to peel the tough outer layer of each stalk of celery. Cut the celery into small pieces (about ¼"). Put the pieces into a large bowl.

▶ Measure the cranberries and add them to the bowl.

▶ Use clean scissors to cut the dried plums into small pieces.

▶ Snip the chives with clean scissors into tiny pieces (if using).

▶ Add the cranberries, dried plums, and chives to the bowl. Dice the turkey into ¼–½" cubes. Add them to the mixture in the bowl. Measure yogurt and add to the turkey mixture.

▶ Using clean hands, a spoon, or a spatula, stir the salad ingredients together until coated in yogurt. Season to taste with salt and pepper.

▶ To serve, scoop some of the turkey mixture and put inside a pita pocket. Add some lettuce for extra color and crunch, and enjoy.

▶ Store leftovers in a covered container in the refrigerator for up to 3 days.

# R & B Chili

**Serves 6**

The midday meal helps fuel our children for the rest of their busy day. The rice and bean combination is a complete protein and takes a traditionally meaty chili in a different direction. Make it fun for your kids. Pack the chili in a thermos along with some delicious toppings and tortilla chips in reusable containers on the side.

- ☐ ½ cup dried black beans, or 1 cup canned
- ☐ ½ cup dried pinto beans, or 1 cup canned
- ☐ 1 red onion
- ☐ 2 carrots
- ☐ 1 stalk celery, organic if possible
- ☐ 1 red bell pepper, organic if possible
- ☐ 1 green bell pepper, organic if possible
- ☐ 3 tablespoons olive oil
- ☐ 3 cloves garlic
- ☐ 1 cup brown rice, short grain

- ☐ 2 (15-ounce) cans diced tomatoes, organic if possible (If you like a little extra spiciness, use fire-roasted with green chiles)
- ☐ 2 cups water
- ☐ 1 tablespoon chili powder
- ☐ 1 tablespoon cumin
- ☐ 1 teaspoon salt
- ☐ Optional toppings: plain yogurt, sour cream, grated sharp Cheddar cheese, cilantro leaves

**2-3** | **4-6** | **7-10** | **11+**

▶ If you are using dried beans, soak them overnight, drain them, and then cook them until they are tender.

▶ Dice the red onion.

▶ Wash the carrots, celery, and bell peppers in cool water.

▶ Dice the carrots and celery.

▶ Heat the oil in a Dutch oven or covered pot over medium-high heat.

▶ Add the onions and cook, stirring occasionally, for 7 minutes or until they start to turn brown.

- ▶ Add the carrots and celery and continue cooking for another 5 minutes.

- ▶ Dice the bell peppers.

- ▶ Peel the paper skin from the garlic.

- ▶ Mash the garlic with a garlic press or dice it finely with a sharp knife.

- ▶ Add it to the pot and stir for about 30 seconds.

- ▶ Add the bell peppers to the pot and stir.

- ▶ Measure the brown rice.

- ▶ Add the brown rice to the pot and stir to combine all of the ingredients.

- ▶ If you are using canned beans, drain and rinse them over a colander in the sink.

- ▶ Add the beans and 2 cups of water to the pot.

- ▶ Open the cans of tomatoes. Pour the tomatoes, along with their juice, into the pot.

- ▶ Measure and add the chili powder, cumin, and salt to the other ingredients.

- ▶ Bring to a boil. Once it is boiling, cover and reduce to a simmer for an hour.

- ▶ Remove the lid and simmer for an additional 20 minutes.

- ▶ If desired, top with plain yogurt, sour cream, shredded sharp Cheddar cheese, and/or minced cilantro.

# Croque Monsieur

*Adapted with permission from my friend and fellow IACP member, Belinda Smith-Sullivan.*

**Serves 4**

Leave it to the French to turn something as simple as a sandwich into a unique mouthwatering experience. The Croque Monsieur (pronounced croak miss-yer), which means "crisp mister," is a classic in Parisian cafes and throughout France. The Croque—as it is referred to—is simply a ham and cheese sandwich fried in butter. So you are probably wondering what makes it so special. It's the frying in butter that transforms this sandwich into a golden brown delight oozing with warm melted cheese. Serve it with a fried egg on top and it becomes a Croque Madame. Add turkey or chicken and you have a Monte Cristo.

- ☐ 1 loaf round crusty French bread
- ☐ 4 slices Gruyère cheese
- ☐ 3 tablespoons butter, as needed
- ☐ 2 tablespoons Dijon mustard, as needed
- ☐ 8 slices baked ham

**2-3    4-6    7-10    11+**

▶ Slice the bread if it is not already sliced.

▶ Slice 4 generous slices of cheese.

▶ Soften or melt the butter in the microwave or on the stove.

▶ For each sandwich, spread Dijon mustard on one side of two slices of bread.

▶ Add 2 slices of ham and 1 slice of cheese per sandwich.

▶ Generously butter the outside of each sandwich on both sides.

▶ Heat a large skillet or double-burner griddle, coated with cooking spray, on medium-high heat.

▶ Add the sandwiches and cook for 3–4 minutes on each side or until golden brown.

# GOING GREEN
## Field of Dreams:
## Pasture-Raised Animals

The meat industry is a controversial one, and I'll admit that I spent more than twenty years of my life avoiding it on principle. Factory farms aren't kind to animals and they produce gobs of pollution. Those two reasons alone are more than enough to create vegetarians out of some people.

Pastured meat is another story. These animals roam in a natural environment and are able to eat grasses and other plants that their bodies are adapted to eat. If their grazing lands are rotated properly, these animals can also fertilize the ground and maintain a healthy ecosystem. Instead of the producer relying on fossil fuels to transport animal feed and waste, pasture-raised animals feed themselves and spread their own manure.

Another bonus: Research shows that the meat from pastured animals has more vitamins and is lower in fat and calories!

# Wrap It Up: Toga Style

**Serves many!***

Wraps are fun to eat. Not only can you change what's inside, but you can switch out the wrapper too. Tortillas come in a variety of different colors (such as green-colored with spinach, or red-colored with tomato) and can be made out of corn, flour, and a variety of other grains. Corn tortillas, while tasty, aren't the best choice for wrap recipes because they have a tendency to crumble when cold.

*\*Makes as many wraps as you have ingredients for!*

- ☐ Hummus (see the recipe in Chapter 7)
- ☐ Whole wheat flour tortillas
- ☐ Spinach leaves
- ☐ Kalamata olives
- ☐ Cucumber
- ☐ Feta cheese

| 2-3 | 4-6 | 7-10 | 11+ |
|-----|-----|------|-----|

▶ Spread a thin layer of hummus on a tortilla.

▶ Wash and dry the spinach leaves.

▶ Slice the kalamata olives and the cucumber.

▶ Crumble the feta cheese.

▶ Layer the spinach, olives, cucumber, and feta cheese onto the tortilla.

▶ Fold up the side farthest from you.

▶ Roll the tortilla from left to right and place it with the seam side down on your serving plate or in your reusable school lunch container.

## GOING GREEN
### Conserving Our Resources

To conserve energy, wash your produce in cold water. Instead of letting the water pour from the faucet as you rinse your veggies, simply fill your sink with a few inches of water and wash all of the produce for your meal at once.

# Chewy Maple Granola Bars

**Serves 8\***

Can you name one thing that all store-bought granola bars have in common? If you said "packaging," you are right! Each bar is wrapped in a nonrecyclable wrapper and then all of them are bundled together in a cardboard box. All of that packaging takes energy and resources to produce, and it usually all ends up in a landfill. Making your own snacks is one of the easiest ways to use your kitchen to help the planet. By baking granola bars at home, you eliminate the need for wrappers. Instead, you can pack these tasty treats in reusable containers and take them anywhere you go!

*\*The servings depend on how large you cut the bars!*

- ☐ ½ cup butter, melted and cooled
- ☐ ¼ cup honey
- ☐ ¼ cup maple syrup
- ☐ 1 teaspoon vanilla extract
- ☐ 1 egg
- ☐ 2 cups oats (not instant)
- ☐ ½ cup shredded coconut (either sweetened or unsweetened)
- ☐ ¾ cup dried cranberries or blueberries

- ☐ ⅓ cup raisins
- ☐ ¼ teaspoon cinnamon
- ☐ ¼ teaspoon salt
- ☐ ¼ cup flour
- ☐ 2 tablespoons sesame seeds
- ☐ ⅔ cup pecan halves
- ☐ ½ cup chocolate chips, optional

| 2-3 | 4-6 | 7-10 | 11+ |
|-----|-----|------|-----|

▶ Preheat oven to 350°F.

▶ Melt the butter and allow it to cool slightly while you prepare the other ingredients.

▶ Measure honey, maple syrup, and vanilla into a bowl, and stir to combine.

*continued on next page*

## Chewy Maple Granola Bars—continued

▶ Crack the egg over a small bowl. Fish out any stray shells.

▶ Add the egg and butter to the syrup mixture.

▶ Measure oats, coconut, dried berries, raisins, cinnamon, salt, flour, seeds, pecans, and chocolate chips (if using), and pour into a large bowl.

▶ Use clean hands to mix together.

▶ Pour the syrup mixture over the oats mixture.

▶ Use clean hands or two spoons to mix the ingredients together and be sure that the oats are coated in the maple syrup mixture.

▶ Line a 9" square baking pan with two sheets of parchment paper. Be sure you press the paper into the corners.

▶ Spoon the coated oat mixture into the baking pan and press flat, filling the entire pan.

▶ Bake on the lower rack of the oven for 20–25 minutes, until the top is set and starts to turn golden brown.

▶ Remove from the oven and allow to come to room temperature.

▶ Refrigerate for at least an hour before cutting into squares.

▶ Store in an airtight container.

# Salty Pretzel Pillows

**Serves 8**

Science happens everywhere we look . . . and even in some places we don't. The kitchen is an especially wonderful laboratory for this recipe. Not only do you get to observe yeast in action, but you also see chemistry at work when you bathe your pretzel pillows in a baking soda solution before putting them in the oven. Pay particular attention to the golden brown color on your nuggets, which would ordinarily take a much longer baking time to generate. It's not magic—it's kitchen science!

**Pretzel dough:**

- ☐ 1 package active dry yeast (2½ teaspoons)
- ☐ 2 tablespoons brown sugar, light or dark
- ☐ 1½ cups warm water, approximately 110°F
- ☐ 5 tablespoons unsalted butter, melted
- ☐ 2½ teaspoons kosher salt
- ☐ 2½ cups unbleached all-purpose flour
- ☐ 2 cups whole wheat flour
- ☐ Vegetable oil, for the bowl

**To cook:**

- ☐ 10 cups water
- ☐ ⅔ cup baking soda
- ☐ 1 egg yolk, with a splash of water
- ☐ Coarse sea salt
- ☐ Optional toppings: poppy or sesame seeds

**2–3**  **4–6**  **7–10**  **11+**

**To prepare the dough:**

▶ Measure the yeast, brown sugar, and warm water.

▶ Combine them in a large bowl or the bowl of a stand mixer.

▶ Let sit for approximately 5 minutes, or until foamy.

▶ Meanwhile, melt the butter in a skillet over low heat.

▶ Add the butter to the yeast mixture and stir to combine.

*continued*

# Salty Pretzel Pillows—continued

▶ Measure salt and add it to the bowl. Measure the all-purpose flour, and add it to the bowl.

▶ Use a dough hook on your mixer (or a wooden spoon) to slowly stir the ingredients together until combined. Once the flour is incorporated, you can add the whole wheat flour, ½ cup at a time, until it is mixed into the mixture.

▶ Now you can turn up the speed of your mixer and continue stirring until the dough clumps together, and pulls away from the sides of the bowl.

▶ Remove the dough from the bowl, and massage it with your hands into the shape of a ball.

▶ Pour some vegetable oil on a clean cloth and rub the insides of a medium-sized bowl. Put the dough ball inside the bowl, and turn to coat it lightly in the oil.

▶ Cover the bowl and allow the dough to rest for up to an hour. It should rise to approximately double in size.

▶ Preheat the oven to 425°F.

▶ Measure 10 cups water and pour it into a large pot.

▶ Bring the water to a boil. Measure the baking soda and add it to the boiling water.

▶ Spray two or three baking sheets with nonstick cooking spray or wipe them with a towel coated in oil.

▶ Remove the dough from the bowl.

▶ Divide it into 8 equally sized pieces.

▶ Roll each piece into a rope, approximately 12–18" long.

▶ Using a dinner knife or dough scraper, cut the rope of dough into little pieces, each approximately 1" long.

*continued on next page*

# Salty Pretzel Pillows—continued

▶ Using a slotted spoon, add approximately 15–20 pretzel pillows to the boiling water at a time.

▶ Boil briefly, approximately 30 seconds. They will rise to the surface, which makes it easier to scoop them out with the slotted spoon.

▶ Gently transfer the pieces to the prepared trays, making sure that they aren't touching. Repeat until you have used up all of the dough.

▶ Get out two small bowls and crack an egg over one bowl.

▶ Empty the egg into someone's clean hands. Open the fingers slightly, allowing the white to drip through into the bowl below. (Store the white in a covered container in the refrigerator for breakfast tomorrow.) The yolk should remain in the hand.

▶ Put the yolk in the second bowl and add a splash of water.

▶ Stir with a fork to combine.

▶ Using a pastry brush, paint each of the pretzel pillows with the egg-yolk mixture.

▶ Sprinkle with coarse sea salt, and seeds, if desired.

▶ Bake on the center rack of your oven, checking after 10 minutes. They are done when they are golden brown (10–16 minutes).

▶ Allow the pretzels to cool completely before storing at room temperature in an airtight container.

# Chapter 4

## What's for Dinner?

# Chicken Piccata with Linguine

**Serves 4-6** This recipe is one of my family's favorites. It's fresh and light, and it has components that each of our family members enjoys, which helps to keep the peace during dinnertime! Don't forget to read through the steps before you begin. I promise it will save you time and make the recipe a cinch to prepare.

☐ 3 cups fresh spinach leaves

☐ 2 tablespoons lemon juice (from one lemon)

☐ 8 ounces linguine, preferably whole grain

☐ 2 tablespoons butter

☐ Salt and pepper to taste

☐ ½ cup all-purpose flour

☐ 1½ pounds chicken tenderloin (tenders)

☐ 2 tablespoons olive oil

☐ ¾ cup wine, white and dry

☐ 2 tablespoons capers

**2-3**  **4-6**  **7-10**  **11+**

▶ Wash the spinach in a colander inside the sink.

▶ Tear the leaves into small pieces and set aside.

▶ Cut the lemon in half.

▶ Juice the lemon. You can use a juicer, a reamer, or just squeeze it by hand. Be sure to pick out any stray seeds (or pips, as they say in England!). Reserve the juice.

▶ Bring a large pot of salted water to a boil. Cook the linguine until it is still just barely firm in the center (according to package instructions).

- ▶ Before draining the pasta, reserve 1 cup of the cooking water and add spinach to the pot of pasta, making sure that all of the leaves get submerged in the water.

- ▶ Drain pasta and spinach and return to pot.

- ▶ Toss with 1 tablespoon of the butter; season with salt and pepper.

- ▶ Add some reserved pasta water if necessary to prevent the noodles from sticking together.

- ▶ Cover to keep warm.

- ▶ Place flour in a shallow bowl.

- ▶ Sprinkle each chicken tender with salt and pepper and then dip each piece into the flour, flipping over to coat on both sides. Gently shake each tender over the bowl so that the excess flour comes off.

- ▶ In a large skillet, heat 1 tablespoon olive oil over medium-high heat.

- ▶ Add half the chicken to the skillet; cook until lightly browned and opaque throughout, 1–2 minutes per side.

- ▶ Transfer the cooked chicken to a plate; cover with foil to keep warm.

- ▶ Repeat with remaining oil and chicken.

- ▶ Add wine and lemon juice to the same skillet that you used for the chicken. Cook the liquid over medium-high heat, stirring to loosen browned bits. Keep cooking until the liquid has reduced to ⅓ cup, about 4–5 minutes.

- ▶ Swirl in the remaining 1 tablespoon butter until it melts.

- ▶ Scoop out the capers from the jar, put them into a colander, rinse with water, and let them drain.

- ▶ Add capers to the sauce, and season again with salt and pepper to taste.

- ▶ Put the chicken pieces into the skillet with the sauce, so that it heats through and gets coated with sauce.

- ▶ Serve the chicken and sauce on top of the linguine and spinach.

# GOING GREEN
## All Cooped Up

Package labels can make a person crazy. It's no wonder that people get confused at the grocery store when confronted with a refrigerated wall filled with egg cartons. "Free-range" chickens have access to a door leading outside, but are often so overcrowded inside the hen house that they never find their way out the door. "Cage-free" chickens aren't in cages, which might imply that they have ample leg room. Sadly, this usually just means that they are crammed into a hen house without dividers.

Pastured poultry spend their days outside—digging, rolling in the dirt, looking for insects, and eating grasses and other plants in their environment. Because of predators, they are often kept underneath a bottomless structure or are put inside a coop at night. They have no need for medications or hormones, since they are not overcrowded and eat a balanced diet that allows them to grow normally. Their eggs are often brighter in color and much more flavorful than their industrialized cousins. If your grocery store doesn't carry pastured chicken eggs, see if they will order some. If not, try your farmer's market, community garden . . . or maybe even your neighbor.

# Minestrone with White Beans and Kale

**Serves 6**

This hearty soup is just what the doctor ordered at the end of a cold winter day. Not only is it easy to prepare, it is also filled with seasonal ingredients and packed with vitamins, calcium, and fiber. Serve with a loaf of fresh whole grain bread.

- ☐ 2 cloves garlic
- ☐ 1 medium yellow onion
- ☐ 2 bunches kale
- ☐ 1 tablespoon olive oil
- ☐ Coarse salt and ground pepper, to taste
- ☐ 2 tablespoons tomato paste
- ☐ ½ teaspoon dried thyme
- ☐ ½ teaspoon red pepper flakes, optional
- ☐ 2 cans white beans, rinsed and drained (or 3 cups cooked dry white beans)
- ☐ 1 (14.5-ounce) can organic diced tomatoes, in juice
- ☐ Grated Parmesan, for serving

`2-3`  `4-6`  `7-10`  `11+`

▶ Peel the paper skin from the garlic and the onion.

▶ Press the garlic.

▶ Chop the onion into very small pieces.

▶ Rinse and dry the kale.

▶ Holding the thickest part of the kale stem in one hand, rub the fingers from the other hand along the stem to zip off the leaves.

*continued on next page*

# Minestrone with White Beans and Kale—continued

▶ Tear the leaves into pieces and save the stems for your compost or backyard chickens.

▶ In a large saucepan or pot, heat oil over medium. Add the onion to the pot and season with salt and pepper. Cook, stirring occasionally, until onion begins to soften, 5–6 minutes.

▶ Add the garlic to the skillet.

▶ Measure the tomato paste. (See the note.)

▶ Add the tomato paste to the onions. Stir until it is mixed in, coating the onions.

▶ Add the kale to the pot.

▶ Measure the thyme and red pepper flakes, if using.

▶ Add them to the pot and stir until the kale begins to wilt. This should take about 2–3 minutes.

▶ Open the cans of beans or measure your cooked beans.

▶ Drain and rinse the beans in a colander in the kitchen sink. Scoop out about 1 cup of beans and pour them into a medium-sized bowl. Mash them with a potato masher, the back of a spoon, or with clean hands. (The beans help to thicken the soup.)

▶ Add all of the beans to the pot.

▶ Open the can of tomatoes and pour the tomatoes and their juice into the pot.

▶ Use the tomato can to measure 2½ cans of water.

▶ Add the cans of water to the pot. Stir all of the soup ingredients together and bring the soup to a boil.

▶ Reduce the heat, put the cover on the pot, and simmer for about 15 minutes.

▶ Before serving, check to be sure that the kale is tender.

▶ Season with salt and pepper to taste and garnish with grated Parmesan, if desired.

*Note:* You can purchase tomato paste in a tube, just like a tube of toothpaste. Squeeze out what you need and then store the rest. If you can't find tomato paste in a tube, you can buy it in a can. Simply use what you need, and then scoop the rest onto a cookie sheet in 1-tablespoon blobs. Put the cookie sheet in the freezer, and once the blobs have frozen, remove them from the tray and store them in a freezer-safe bag or storage container.

# ☑ RECIPE FOR ACTION
## Helping the Homeless

Sometimes it's the little things that make a difference in someone's day. Other times, though, it takes a collaborative effort. SOUP: The Bowl That Keeps Feeding, was such an endeavor. Studio 4 Art, an art studio for children, partnered with What's Cooking, my cooking school for children, to raise money for the emergency family shelter in our community. Kebby McInroy patiently taught children to throw and glaze soup bowls, while I worked with local schoolchildren to prepare several varieties of soup. At our culminating event, guests paid for lunch, which included a bowl of their choice, filled with soup. Everyone was able to take home their empty soup bowl as a reminder of the chidren in our community who don't always have enough to eat. All proceeds of our event were donated to Homeward Bound of Marin to help local families in crisis.

# Pork Ribs with Asian BBQ Sauce

**Serves 6** Unfortunately this isn't a recipe that you can throw together at the last minute due to the long marinating time. But believe me, it's worth it! Prepare this recipe when you and your kids have a few spare minutes, and then enjoy it for dinner the following night. The good news is that you now have a fantastic make-ahead dish in your arsenal!

- ☐ 4 pounds baby back pork ribs, organic and grass fed, if possible
- ☐ 2 teaspoons onion powder, divided use
- ☐ 2 teaspoons five-spice powder, divided use
- ☐ ½ cup ketchup (select a brand that does not use high-fructose corn syrup)
- ☐ 1 cup hoisin sauce
- ☐ ¼ cup sherry or mirin
- ☐ 4 tablespoons rice vinegar
- ☐ 1 tablespoon sesame oil
- ☐ 1–2 teaspoons ground ginger (adjust to your taste)
- ☐ 2 teaspoons salt
- ☐ Spicy Asian chili sauce, optional, to taste (1 teaspoon to start)

| 2-3 | 4-6 | 7-10 | 11+ |

▶ Before you start, get the equipment you need: Use either a roasting pan that you can cover with foil OR use a large food storage container with a lid. If you don't like to do dishes (who does?), you might want to just use the roasting pan that you will cook the ribs in.

▶ Place the ribs in your container and then wash your hands.

▶ Measure 1 teaspoon onion powder and 1 teaspoon five-spice powder and mix them together in a small bowl. Rub this mixture all over the meat.

▶ Wash your hands!

▶ In a separate bowl, add the ketchup, hoisin sauce, sherry or mirin, rice vinegar, and sesame oil.

▶ Measure 1 teaspoon onion powder, 1 teaspoon five-spice powder, ginger, and salt, and add to the sauce.

▶ If using, add the spicy Asian chili sauce.

▶ Mix the sauce ingredients together.

▶ Pour the sauce over the ribs, turning them to coat completely. Turn the ribs over, and store them with the meat side down.

▶ Cover the container holding the ribs and put into the refrigerator.

▶ Marinate for anywhere between 4–24 hours. You can start them in the morning for dinner that night, or you can leave them in the refrigerator overnight.

▶ On the day that you cook the ribs, remove them from the refrigerator about ½ hour before you want to start cooking.

▶ At the same time, preheat the oven to 400°F with the rack in the center.

▶ Transfer the ribs to a roasting pan, if they are stored in another container, and discard the marinade.

▶ Cover the pan with foil and roast (meat side down) for 30 minutes.

▶ Turn the ribs over, so they have the meat side up.

▶ Roast for an additional 30–35 minutes, basting occasionally with the pan sauces.

▶ When they are finished cooking, allow to cool for a few minutes.

▶ Cut the meat between the bones (with a sharp knife or kitchen shears) to separate the ribs.

## GOING GREEN
## Sustainable Farms

Our nation is filled with farms of all types. Some have gardens and a few chickens running around the back yard. Other farms have thousands of animals, living so close together that they are flank-to-flank. I try to follow my heart and support the farms that consider the health and well-being of their animals, workers, and the physical environment.

Sustainable farms treat their animals humanely. Their animals get lots of fresh air, have the opportunity to graze and socialize, and generally act like animals. These farms care for their workers, paying them a fair wage and making sure that they aren't exposed to hazardous chemicals. They don't spray chemicals on their plants or give their animals medication when they aren't sick. Sustainable farms recycle and compost. Seems like a no-brainer to me. They get your support every time you vote with my fork!

# Grandma's Spaghetti Gravy

**Serves 6-8**

I always felt loved when my grandma fed me. After I left the nest, she would often fill my freezer with matzoh ball soup and this special spaghetti gravy. When she passed away, I asked to be the custodian of her avocado-green recipe box. As I was writing this book, I crossed my fingers and hoped that I might find this recipe tucked away inside. I thought I'd share it with you because it is just too good to keep to myself. When you make it, I bet you'll love the taste too.

- ☐ 1 pound ground turkey or grass-fed beef
- ☐ ½ cup boiling water
- ☐ ¼ ounce dried porcini mushrooms
- ☐ 2 large onions
- ☐ 2 stalks celery
- ☐ 2 tablespoons vegetable oil
- ☐ 1 cup parsley (or a big handful from the garden)
- ☐ 2 cloves garlic
- ☐ 2 carrots
- ☐ 1 (14-ounce) can chopped tomatoes, undrained, organic if possible
- ☐ 3 (14-ounce) cans tomato sauce

**2-3 | 4-6 | 7-10 | 11+**

▶ Preheat the oven to 300°F.

▶ Brown the meat over medium-high heat on the stove.

▶ Meanwhile, pour boiling water over the dried mushrooms in a heat-proof bowl. Allow the mushrooms to soften for several minutes.

▶ Set a colander over a bowl and pour the meat into it to drain off the fat. When the fat cools, dump it into the trash. Set the meat aside.

▶ Peel the paper skin from the onions.

▶ Dice the onions and celery and sauté them in vegetable oil.

*continued on next page*

## Grandma's Spaghetti Gravy—continued

▶ Pick the parsley leaves from the stem.

▶ Peel the paper skin from the garlic.

▶ Finely chop the carrots, parsley, and garlic, and add them to the onions when they have turned golden brown.

▶ Remove the softened mushrooms from the water, making sure to save the flavored water. Chop the mushrooms and add them to the cooking vegetable mixture.

▶ Pour the reserved mushroom water (being careful not to add the dirt bits at the bottom), canned chopped tomatoes (with their liquid), tomato sauce, and two cans of water into a large roasting pan.

▶ Add the cooked meat and vegetables to the roasting pan.

▶ Stir all of the sauce ingredients so that they are mixed together.

▶ Cover the roasting pan and cook for 2 hours.

▶ Carefully remove the roasting pan from the oven, uncover, and simmer on the stovetop for another hour to thicken the gravy.

▶ Serve over pasta.

☑ **RECIPE FOR ACTION**

## Providing Comfort with a Warm Meal

When we hear about a friend having a baby, we often take a meal to the new family. While doing this usually is an excuse to see their new addition, it nourishes the parents and allows them to spend time bonding with the baby instead of cooking. It's especially wonderful when we can cook for families who are blessed with good news, but it might be even more meaningful to cook for a family in crisis. When a family member is ill or in the hospital, people are unlikely thinking about what to make for dinner. Recruit the kids, plan a delicious meal, and deliver some edible love to your friends.

# Biscuit-Topped Chicken Potpie

**Serves 4–6**

As parents, most of us are qualified to be jugglers in the circus! Between work, kids, afterschool activities, and play dates, it is hard to spend as much time in the kitchen as you might like. Just because potpies are traditionally served with a pie crust, that doesn't mean we have time to make them that way. The biscuit topping in this recipe is a great shortcut to this otherwise labor-intensive dish. And if you are really desperate for time, you can even use a store-bought rotisserie chicken and cut up veggies from your store's salad bar!

**Potpie filling:**

☐ 2 tablespoons olive oil

☐ 1 pound chicken breast meat, bone-in (you can also use boneless/skinless if you wish)

☐ Salt, to taste

☐ Lemon pepper, to taste (you can substitute black pepper)

☐ 2 stalks celery, organic if possible

☐ 3 or 4 carrots

☐ 1 yellow onion

☐ 5 tablespoons butter

☐ 2 tablespoons olive oil

☐ 2 cups frozen peas

☐ ½ cup unbleached all-purpose flour

☐ 4 cups chicken broth

**Biscuit topping:**

☐ 2 cups unbleached all-purpose flour

☐ ¼ teaspoon salt

☐ 1 teaspoon sugar

☐ 1 tablespoon baking powder

☐ ½ teaspoon baking soda

☐ 2 teaspoons fresh thyme leaves

☐ 6 tablespoons cold unsalted butter

☐ ¾ cup low-fat milk or buttermilk

*continued on next page*

# Biscuit-Topped Chicken Potpie—continued

`2-3` `4-6` `7-10` `11+`

▶ Preheat the oven to 350°F.

**Prepare the filling:**

▶ Measure 2 tablespoons of olive oil and rub it onto the chicken. Wash your hands.

▶ Sprinkle each piece of chicken with salt and lemon pepper.

▶ Roast chicken for 35 minutes or until juices run clear when pierced with a knife.

▶ Remove chicken from the oven and set aside to cool.

▶ Meanwhile, rinse the celery and carrots.

▶ Peel the celery with a vegetable peeler, saving the peels for your compost or chickens. Peel the paper skin from the onions.

▶ Dice the celery, carrots, and onions into pea-sized pieces. (You should cut a thin slice from the side of each carrot for your kids so it lays flat on the cutting surface without rolling around as they cut it.)

▶ Heat butter and 2 tablespoons of olive oil in a skillet over medium-high heat.

▶ Sauté the onions for 10 minutes, or until they turn translucent.

▶ Add the carrots and celery to the onions, stir, and cook for an additional 3 minutes.

▶ When the chicken has finished cooking and is cool enough to handle, remove the skin and pull the meat from the bones.

▶ Dice the chicken and add it to the skillet with the vegetable mixture.

▶ Measure frozen peas and add them to the skillet.

▶ Measure the flour, add to the vegetable mixture, and stir to coat.

▶ Measure the broth and add it slowly to the skillet, stirring constantly.

▶ The flour in the broth will help to thicken the sauce. This should take less than 5 minutes.

**Prepare the biscuit topping:**

▶ Increase oven temperature to 400°F.

▶ Measure the flour, salt, sugar, baking powder, and baking soda, and pour them into a large bowl.

▶ Run your pinched fingers along the stem of the thyme to pop the leaves off. Measure 2 teaspoons of leaves. Add to the flour mixture.

▶ Whisk the dry ingredients gently to combine. (Note: If you stir too fast, it will poof all over the kitchen!)

▶ Cut the cold butter into pea-sized pieces with a child-safe knife.

▶ Add the butter to the flour mixture.

▶ Using clean hands, massage the butter into the dry ingredients until it all becomes crumbly.

▶ Measure the milk and add it to the dry ingredients, then use a fork to stir the ingredients together until they come together into a sticky dough.

**To assemble:**

▶ Taste the filling one more time. It might need more salt. If so, add what you like, stir, and taste again.

▶ You can either prepare individual potpies, or one large one to serve family style. If using multiple dishes, divide the filling among them using a soup ladle. Whatever you decide to bake your pies in, make sure it's oven-safe.

▶ Drop the biscuit batter in dollops by the spoonful all over the top of the filling. It does not need to completely cover the topping.

▶ Bake the potpies for 20 minutes, until top is golden brown and filling is bubbly.

*Note:* Did you notice I asked you to peel the celery, but not the carrots? Carrot peels contain lots of vitamins, so if you know that your carrots were grown in healthy soil, just leave the skin on (after a good washing, of course). Celery, on the other hand, has a fibrous outer layer that is very difficult to cut and chew. You can easily remove it with a swipe or two from your vegetable peeler.

# Wish-for-a-Fish Pasta

**Serves 4-6**

Everyone needs a go-to recipe that they can prepare at the last minute from ingredients in the pantry. Recipes like this save money because they are less expensive than takeout, and they keep you in control of the ingredients, which keeps the family healthier. Try to look for tuna that has been pole-caught. This technique doesn't harm other marine critters and usually yields smaller fish that contain fewer toxins.

- ☐ 1 pound pasta, penne, or fusilli
- ☐ 1 lemon
- ☐ 3 (6-ounce) cans albacore tuna (packed in oil, undrained, pole-caught)
- ☐ 3 tablespoons fresh parsley or chives
- ☐ Salt and black pepper, to taste
- ☐ Parmesan cheese (optional), to taste

**2-3  4-6  7-10  11+**

▶ Put a large pot of salted water on the stove to boil. Cook the package of pasta according to the directions.

▶ In the meantime, wash the lemon.

▶ Zest lemon with a lemon zester or with a microplane. Cut lemon in half and squeeze the juice into a serving bowl.

▶ Open the cans of tuna.

▶ Drain the oil from two of the cans of tuna down the drain and empty the contents from all 3 cans into serving bowl.

▶ Use a fork to break up the tuna into small flakes.

▶ Rinse the herbs and pat them dry with a clean dishcloth.

▶ If you are using parsley, pick the leaves from the stem. Snip the herbs into small pieces with clean scissors. (Older children or adults can use a knife, of course.)

▶ Add the herbs to the serving bowl with the tuna and lemon.

▶ When the pasta has finished cooking, drain it in a colander in the sink and pour the hot pasta into the serving bowl.

▶ Mix the pasta with the tuna and lemon mixture so that the noodles are evenly coated. The heat from the noodles will cause some of the flavors in the herbs to infuse into the pasta. Season with salt and pepper, and add Parmesan cheese, to taste, if desired.

## GOING GREEN
## Not All Tuna Is Created Equal:
# What's the Catch?

Lots of parents ask me how to navigate the grocery store aisle and select the "best" canned tuna on the shelves. Some parents worry about toxins and others fear that if they make the wrong choices, tuna will go the way of the dodo. As you might expect, there is a ton of information "out there" but most of it is scientific gibberish and is difficult for the average overextended parent to translate.

**The lowdown on sustainability:**

- The way that tuna is harvested matters. Some fishing techniques are easier for the fishermen, but accidentally kill lots of other creatures, like dolphins, sea turtles, and marine birds. The best fishing technique is called "pole-caught." Picture a guy in yellow waterproof overalls at the back of the boat with a fishing pole. They are looking for albacore and release everything else. Enough said.
- "Long lines" are particularly lethal—they trail behind the boat, sometimes for miles, with hooks and lures all along their entire length. Yes, they catch tuna. But they also catch lots of other marine animals that happen to get hooked or tangled.
- Bigeye and bluefin tuna are endangered. Do not order them if you see them on a restaurant menu. You are voting with your fork—and if you pay for something you don't agree with, it will keep happening.

**The lowdown on health:**

- Smaller, younger fish have fewer toxins accumulated in their bodies. So it makes sense that these fish contain lower levels of mercury and PCBs and are healthier to eat.
- Albacore that are pole-caught are young fish that forage closer to the surface. This is the healthiest choice!
- Albacore that are caught on long lines are much larger fish, living in deeper water. Fish living in deep waters are larger and older, and have had more time to accumulate toxins in their bodies. Imagine a dash of toxins in every fish it eats over a whole lifetime. It makes for a toxic fish, and one best avoided.

# Pork Chops with Sage Butter

**Serves 4**

When I was a child, I attended summer camp at our local Humane Society. Back in those days, they educated kids about animal cruelty by frightening us. It sure worked—I didn't eat meat for more than twenty years after that. But when I got older and started to get to know the farmers who grew my food, I learned that animals can be raised naturally, grazing and helping the fertility of the land. Many thanks to Prather Ranch for raising happy pigs that I can eat without feeling like I am encouraging a misdirected industry.

- ☐ ¼ cup sage leaves (about a handful)
- ☐ ½ stick salted butter, softened
- ☐ 1 clove garlic
- ☐ ¼ lemon, juiced (optional)
- ☐ Salt and black pepper, to taste
- ☐ 4 pork chops, ½" thick
- ☐ 1–2 tablespoons olive oil (for the pan)

2-3 | 4-6 | 7-10 | 11+

**Prepare the sage butter:**

▶ Pick the sage leaves from the stems and measure ¼ cup.

▶ Mince them finely.

▶ Melt 1 tablespoon of the butter in a skillet. Add minced sage to the melted butter and allow to simmer for 2–4 minutes. Remove the pan from the heat.

▶ Meanwhile, peel the paper skin from the garlic.

▶ Press the garlic with a garlic press and add it to the warm sage mixture.

▶ Allow the sage mixture to cool for several minutes.

▶ Add the sage to the remaining softened butter and stir to combine.

▶ If desired, add lemon juice, salt, and pepper.

**Prepare the pork chops:**

▶ Season the pork chops with salt and pepper on both sides. Wash hands.

▶ Heat a heavy frying pan over medium-high heat. Add 1–2 tablespoons olive oil, or enough to lightly coat the pan.

▶ Sear the pork chops for 3 minutes on the first side. Turn the pork over and allow to cook for 2 minutes and then turn off the heat. The meat will continue cooking in the pan.

▶ Using an instant-read thermometer, take the temperature of the meat. The internal temperature should be 160°F when it is finished.

▶ Spread a dollop of the sage butter on the hot chops. The heat of the chops will melt the butter and release the fragrance of the sage. Mmmm. Delicious!

# Sorrel-icious Sole

**Serves 4**

When I was growing up, my mother would often make fillet of sole with a sorrel-butter sauce, using the large green sorrel leaves from the garden. Its lemony flavor was a perfect balance with the mild flavor of the white fish. When I planted our new garden beds at the end of winter, I made sure to buy a sorrel plant from Chicory, my vegetable seedling vendor at the farmer's market. It has grown into a plant to be reckoned with, and when I brainstormed this recipe with my friend Tanya, our goal was to take advantage of my bumper crop.

☐ 4 tablespoons mayonnaise

☐ 2 tablespoons extra-virgin olive oil

☐ 1 clove garlic

☐ 1 cup sorrel leaves

☐ ¼ teaspoon salt

☐ ¾ cup panko (Japanese bread crumbs)

☐ 1 pound sole fillets

| 2–3 | 4–6 | 7–10 | 11+ |

▶ Preheat the oven to 400°F.

▶ Line a sheet pan with a Silpat (reusable silicone mat) or parchment paper.

▶ Put a cooling rack over your kitchen sink and spray it with nonstick spray, or wipe it with a cloth dipped in oil.

▶ Set the rack over the sheet pan. Set aside until you are ready to cook the fish.

**To prepare the sorrel sauce:**

▶ Measure the mayonnaise and olive oil and pour into the blender.

▶ Peel the paper skin from the garlic and add the garlic to the blender. If you wish, you can smash the garlic with the back of a small skillet first.

▶ Tear the sorrel leaves away from the rib down the center.

▶ Tear the leaves into large chunks until you have enough to fill a 1-cup measuring cup. (Put the ribs in your compost or feed them to your chickens.)

▶ Add the leaves to the blender.

▶ Turn on the blender and purée the ingredients. You may have to turn the blender off and scrape down the sides, so that the ingredients are close to the blades.

**To prepare the fish:**

▶ Measure the panko bread crumbs and pour them on a dinner plate.

▶ Spread 1 tablespoon of the sorrel sauce on each piece of fish.

▶ Press each piece of fish, sauce side down, into the panko bread crumbs. Make sure you press down on the fish, so that the bread crumbs stick to the sauce.

▶ Carefully lift each piece of fish and place it, bread-crumb side up, on the prepared rack. Wash your hands.

▶ Once all of the pieces of fish are prepared, place the tray and cooling rack into the oven.

▶ Cook for 13–20 minutes, or until your fish is done. Cooking time will depend on the thickness of your fish. The fish is finished cooking when it is opaque and firm to the touch.

## GOING GREEN
## Spill the Beans: Spring Gardening

Toward the end of winter, we anxiously count the days until the last frost so that we can get our spring vegetable gardens started. In the meantime, use some of that energy to do a bit of spring cleaning. Gather your young gardeners and have them pull weeds, clear debris, and turn your compost pile.

The early bird gets the worm (or in this case, the veggies). Cabbage and lettuce can handle a light frost, so they are ideal for the impatient gardener who just can't wait. As soon as you can dig in the garden and turn the soil, you can put in your peas and onions. Later in the season, you can plant bush or pole beans, cucumbers, peppers, squash, strawberries, and tomatoes.

# Greek Shrimp with Feta

**Serves 4**

When I talked to my friends about their children's eating habits, they had definite opinions about shrimp. Kids either love them or avoid them like mad. For families that adore the mild and sweet flavor of shrimp, this recipe is made even better with cherry tomatoes picked at their peak. To ensure that our fisheries remain sustainable, please avoid buying "imported" shrimp that comes from outside of North America.

- ☐ 3 scallions
- ☐ ½ red onion
- ☐ 3 tablespoons extra-virgin olive oil
- ☐ 3 cloves garlic
- ☐ 1 (14-ounce) can diced tomatoes, with juice, or 1 pound fresh cherry tomatoes
- ☐ ½ cup white wine, or dry vermouth
- ☐ 1 teaspoon kosher salt
- ☐ ½ teaspoon freshly ground black pepper
- ☐ 1 bunch fresh Italian flat leaf parsley
- ☐ 24 uncooked shrimp, peeled and deveined
- ☐ ½ teaspoon dried oregano
- ☐ 5 ounces feta cheese

**2-3** | 4-6 | **7-10** | **11+**

▶ Use clean scissors to snip the scallions into small pieces. Peel the paper skin from the onion.

▶ Use a knife to finely dice the onion.

▶ Heat oil in an ovenproof skillet over medium heat.

▶ Cook the onion and scallions for 4–5 minutes, stirring occasionally.

▶ Peel the paper skin from the garlic and mash with a garlic press.

▶ Add the garlic to the skillet and stir for another 2 minutes.

▶ Open the can of tomatoes, but don't drain them. Add the tomatoes and their juice to the skillet.

**OR**

▶ If you are using fresh cherry tomatoes, slice each in half and add them to the skillet.

▶ Measure the wine and add it to the skillet. Add salt and pepper, to taste.

▶ Reduce the heat to low and simmer, uncovered, for 10 minutes.

▶ Preheat the broiler.

▶ Pick the parsley leaves from the stem.

▶ Tear the parsley leaves into small pieces.

▶ Add the shrimp, parsley leaves, and oregano to the skillet. Cover and cook for an additional 3 minutes.

▶ Crumble the feta cheese with clean fingers and sprinkle it on top of the shrimp mixture.

▶ Place the skillet under the broiler to melt and brown the feta. Keep an eye on it—it should only take about 2 minutes.

▶ Remove from the oven and serve. This is delicious served over creamy polenta or tossed with cooked pasta.

## GOING GREEN
### Cream of the Crop:
# Summer Gardening

Summertime is the simplest time of year to plant veggies, even if you only have the space for a pot or two. Given the right conditions, your plants will thrive and will inexpensively provide fresh, nutritious goodies for your family. Unfortunately, your plants might also be feeding a variety of pests. Instead of using chemical deterrents for these critters, creatively reuse items from your kitchen. Pesky snails and slugs have sensitive bodies and will be unlikely to cross a ring of crushed eggshells that you have sprinkled as a barrier around the plant. (Some gardeners have better luck with this method than others—maybe city folks have tougher snails?)

At the same time that your vegetables are flourishing, so are the weeds. To prevent their seeds from impregnating your fertile garden soil, smother them with mulch or recycled newspaper topped with straw or compost.

# Summertime Kabobs with Udon Noodles

**Serves 4–6**

Maybe it's because we have seen one too many cooking shows on television, but it seems that when most people talk about using the grill, it's all about meat. This fresh and seasonal recipe is ideal for the grill, as long as you use extra-firm tofu. The marinade, which doubles as an ingredient for the udon noodles, offers an amazing rich flavor, so you'll never miss the meat in tonight's meal!

- ☐ ½ cup mirin (sweet rice wine)
- ☐ ½ cup soy sauce, reduced sodium
- ☐ 2 tablespoons sesame oil
- ☐ ½" chunk gingerroot
- ☐ 1 package extra-firm tofu
- ☐ 2 small zucchini
- ☐ 2 small yellow squash, about 6" long
- ☐ 10–20 button mushrooms, or baby shiitakes, as desired
- ☐ 3 cups vegetable broth, low sodium
- ☐ 12–16 ounces udon noodles
- ☐ 1 red bell pepper
- ☐ 1 handful cilantro or parsley, if desired
- ☐ 2 tablespoons sesame seeds, toasted

| 2-3 | 4-6 | 7-10 | 11+ |

▶ Measure mirin, soy sauce, and sesame oil, and pour them into a medium-sized bowl.

▶ Use a vegetable peeler to peel the skin from the gingerroot.

▶ Use a fine grater or microplane to grate the peeled section of gingerroot.

▶ Add the grated gingerroot to the marinade in the bowl. You may need to scrape the back of the grater to collect the ginger.

*continued*

# Summertime Kabobs with Udon Noodles—continued

▶ Open the tofu and drain out the liquid into the sink. Cut the tofu into 1" squares and add the tofu to the marinade.

▶ Allow the tofu to sit in the marinade for 10 minutes or up to several hours in the refrigerator. Occasionally stir to coat.

▶ Preheat your grill to medium-high heat.

▶ If you are using wooden skewers, soak them in water before using. This will prevent them from burning on the grill.

▶ Slice the zucchini and yellow squash into rounds, approximately ¾" thick.

▶ Wipe the mushrooms clean with a damp cloth.

▶ Remove the tofu from the marinade. Drain the marinade into a pot and reserve while you assemble the kabobs.

▶ Thread the tofu and vegetable pieces onto the skewers. Any pattern is fine—but it helps to use a piece of squash or mushroom on the ends to hold the tofu in place.

▶ Before you cook the kabobs, use tongs to hold a cloth or paper towel to spread a little vegetable spray on the grates of the grill.

▶ Put the kabobs onto the grill. Cook them for 5 minutes, then turn and cook for 5 minutes more.

▶ While the kabobs are cooking, measure 3 cups of vegetable broth into the pot with the reserved tofu marinade.

▶ Bring the liquid to a boil and add the noodles. Cook according to the package directions. (If you are using prepared udon noodles from your local Asian market, they simply need to heat through.)

▶ Wash the bell pepper.

▶ Slice it into very thin slices (julienne style).

▶ If using, pick the cilantro or parsley leaves from the stems and tear them into tiny pieces.

▶ Serve the noodles in individual bowls, topped with broth.

▶ On the top of each bowl of noodles, sprinkle bell pepper slices, sesame seeds, and cilantro or parsley, if desired.

▶ For a beautiful presentation, lay the kabobs across the top of the bowl.

# Taco Salad

**Serves 4-6**

I have always loved the expression, "It takes a village." It usually refers to raising a family, but I find that it applies to almost everything, even cooking. At first, I learned to cook by watching my mother. Now, I learn from celebrities on television and from my numerous virtual friends through their blogs, tweets, and Facebook posts. For example, I learned from my friend Lydia that chili powder is made from chile peppers, blended with a variety of other spices, including oregano, cumin, garlic, paprika, and sometimes cayenne pepper. Learning little tidbits like this helps me to understand the flavors in my food and makes the meal even more special.

☐ ½ cup salsa

☐ ½ cup sour cream, organic if possible

☐ 3 cloves garlic

☐ 1 medium onion

☐ 1 teaspoon canola oil

☐ 1 pound ground turkey

☐ 1 (14-ounce) can black beans, rinsed

☐ 2 teaspoons ground cumin

☐ 2 teaspoons chili powder

☐ 1 teaspoon salt

☐ ¼ cup cilantro, chopped

☐ 8 cups shredded romaine lettuce

☐ ½ cup shredded Cheddar cheese

☐ 2 large plum tomatoes, diced

☐ Optional additions: corn (cut from the cob, thawed frozen, or drained canned), sliced black olives, and crumbled tortilla chips

| 2-3 | 4-6 | 7-10 | 11+ |

▶ Measure and combine salsa and sour cream in a large bowl.

▶ Peel the paper skin from the garlic. Mash or press with a garlic press.

▶ Peel the paper skin from the onion. Dice the onion.

▶ Heat the oil in a large nonstick skillet over medium heat.

▶ Add onion and garlic and cook, stirring often, until softened, about 2 minutes.

- ▶ Add the ground turkey and cook, stirring often and crumbling with a wooden spoon, until cooked through, about 5 minutes.

- ▶ While the turkey cooks, drain the beans in a colander over the sink, and rinse thoroughly.

- ▶ Add cumin, chili powder, and salt to the skillet with the turkey; cook, stirring, to heat through.

- ▶ Remove from the heat.

- ▶ Pour the beans, cilantro, and ½ cup of the salsa mixture into the skillet and stir gently.

- ▶ In a large salad bowl, add lettuce and the remaining salsa mixture, tossing to coat.

- ▶ Add the turkey mixture to the lettuce and toss to combine.

- ▶ Sprinkle with cheese, diced tomatoes, and any optional ingredients that your family enjoys.

## KID ZONE
## It's Hot in the Kitchen

Have you ever noticed that some salsas are mild, while others are spicy? Many include chile peppers, which lend heat and a wonderful flavor to the recipe. The spiciness level of peppers is measured in Scovilles, with bell peppers scoring a zero and the Scotch Bonnet ranking between 100,000 and 350,000!

It's best to wear latex gloves while you are cutting spicy peppers so that you can protect your skin from the oils of the pepper. Be sure not to touch your body with the peppery gloves. Save your itching and scratching until you take the gloves off.

If your mouth feels like it is on fire after you eat something spicy, don't reach for a glass of water. Instead, have a glass of milk, a few spoonfuls of yogurt, or a slice of bread. They will soothe the burn and make you feel better.

# Acorn Squash and Wild Rice Bowls

**Serves 4**

We have the same set of dishes that we received as a wedding gift, fourteen years ago. Every now and again, a new dish makes it into our collection, but it is usually a bowl made by one of our kids. Imagine the family's surprise when I served this meal in something new entirely—an edible bowl made from the acorn squash itself. What a great way to reuse and recycle in the kitchen!

- ☐ 2 acorn squash
- ☐ 2 cloves garlic
- ☐ 1 shallot
- ☐ ½ teaspoon dried sage
- ☐ Salt and pepper, to taste
- ☐ 2 tablespoons butter or olive oil
- ☐ 1 cup wild rice
- ☐ 3 cups water or broth, according to wild rice package directions
- ☐ ¾ pound ground Italian turkey sausage, optional
- ☐ ½ cup dried cherries or cranberries
- ☐ ½ cup pecans, chopped

| 2-3 | 4-6 | 7-10 | 11+ |

▶ Preheat oven to 450°F.

▶ Cut each squash in half, lengthwise.

▶ Use a spoon to scrape out the seeds. If you have backyard chickens or a compost pile, be sure not to throw these away!

▶ Place the squash halves on a baking sheet with the cut side down. Cover tightly with foil.

- Roast until you can easily pierce each squash with the tip of a knife. This should take about 30–40 minutes.

- While the squash cooks, peel the papery skin from the garlic.

- Use a garlic press to mash the garlic.

- Put the garlic in a small bowl.

- Peel the papery skin from the shallot.

- Dice the shallot into tiny pieces.

- Add the pieces to the bowl with the garlic.

- Measure sage and add it to the garlic and shallots. Add a pinch of salt and a grind or two of pepper.

- Heat the butter or olive oil in a large saucepan.

- Add garlic, shallots, sage, salt, and pepper to the pan. Cook, stirring occasionally, until the shallots are tender.

- Measure the rice. Measure water or broth (the rice package or bulk bin will tell you how much you need for the amount of rice you are making).

- Add rice and liquid to the skillet with the garlic mixture and bring to a simmer.

- Cover and cook until the liquid is absorbed, about 25 minutes.

- If you choose to use some ground Italian sausage in the filling, squeeze it from the casings.

- Cook it in a skillet while the rice is cooking.

- While the rice is cooking, measure cherries or cranberries and pecans.

- Remove the rice from heat and add the cherries or cranberries, pecans, and sausage (if using).

- Season with salt and pepper to taste.

- Sprinkle the inside of each squash with salt and pepper.

- Scoop the rice mixture into the squash halves and serve.

# Falling for Fall Quesadillas

**Serves 4**

I'm not sure about you, but I definitely don't have time to be a short-order cook, making separate meals for different members of my family. This recipe is perfect for families with varying taste preferences. With hardly any effort, you can make slight modifications to accommodate the needs of even your strongest critics.

- ☐ ¾ pound button, cremini, or shiitake mushrooms
- ☐ 1½ pounds sweet potatoes
- ☐ 1 tablespoon cumin, ground
- ☐ 5 tablespoons olive oil, divided use
- ☐ Salt and pepper, to taste
- ☐ 1 small onion

- ☐ 8 ounces ground spicy turkey sausage or chorizo (traditional or soy)
- ☐ 6 ounces Monterey jack cheese
- ☐ 6 whole wheat tortillas
- ☐ Tomato salsa, optional

| 2-3 | 4-6 | 7-10 | 11+ |

▶ Preheat oven to 400°F.

▶ Wipe mushrooms clean with a damp cloth. Break off the mushroom stems.

▶ Peel the sweet potatoes. Save the peels and mushroom stems for your chickens or the compost bin.

▶ Cut the sweet potatoes into 1" cubes.

▶ Place the mushrooms and sweet potatoes in a large bowl.

▶ Measure cumin and 2 tablespoons olive oil, and add them to the veggies. Mix the veggies, spices, and oil together with clean hands. Sprinkle with salt and pepper.

▶ Spread the vegetable mixture onto two rimmed baking sheets, so they are not crowded.

▶ Roast the vegetables for 40 minutes, rotating the baking sheets halfway through.

▶ While the veggies are roasting, peel the paper skin from the onion.

- Mince the onion finely.

- Heat a skillet over medium-high heat and add the 2 tablespoons olive oil. Add the ground sausage and onion and sauté until cooked through and lightly browned.

- Put the cooked sausage and onion into the mixing bowl.

- Remove the vegetables from the oven and carefully scoop them back into the mixing bowl.

- Grate the cheese and reserve to use in a few moments.

- Lay 3 tortillas on each baking sheet.

- Divide the roasted vegetables among the 6 tortillas.

- Spread the vegetables gently over half of each tortilla.

- Top the veggies with the sausage and onions.

- Sprinkle the cheese on top of the sausage.

- Fold each tortilla in half and press to close.

- Brush the top of each tortilla with the remaining olive oil.

- Return the baking sheets to the oven.

- Cook for a total of 15 minutes, rotating the trays halfway through.

- They are finished cooking when the cheese has melted and the tortillas are golden brown.

- Using kitchen shears or a pizza cutter, slice each quesadilla into wedges.

- Serve with salsa if desired.

## GOING GREEN
## Dirt Cheap: Fall Gardening

Gardening doesn't have to be expensive. You can purchase seeds and sow them yourself instead of buying more costly seedlings. Perennial edibles, such as rhubarb, asparagus, chives, oregano, or thyme, grow for several seasons, without the added expense or effort of purchasing and planting them every year.

# Pumpkin Ravioli

 **Serves 2–4** Maybe kids love individual packets of food, like raviolis, pot stickers, spring rolls, and calzones because they remind them of presents. Regardless of the reason, the perk is that children are enthusiastic about their food. Instead of buying premade dried raviolis, these are fresh and fun to assemble. Once you have the technique down, try using other seasonal ingredients. For a dessert twist, fill the wrappers with something sweet and pan-fry them in a little butter.

- ☐ 1 cup Puréed Pumpkin (see Chapter 7)
- ☐ ½ cup ricotta cheese
- ☐ ⅓ cup grated Parmesan cheese
- ☐ ¼ teaspoon salt
- ☐ ¼ teaspoon white pepper
- ☐ Optional: sage, rosemary, or any of your other favorite herbs, to taste
- ☐ 10–15 wonton wrappers
- ☐ 2 cups vegetable or chicken broth
- ☐ Fresh Italian flat leaf parsley, to taste
- ☐ 2 tablespoons olive oil

**2-3**  4-6  **7-10**  **11+**

▶ Measure the puréed pumpkin and ricotta cheese, and pour them into a small mixing bowl.

▶ Grate the Parmesan into the bowl.

▶ Add salt and pepper and stir to combine. If desired, add a pinch of your favorite minced herbs to the filling.

*continued on next page*

## Pumpkin Ravioli—continued

▶ If you are using a dumpling press, open it flat and place the wonton wrapper in the center. Otherwise, place your wrapper on a clean work surface.

▶ Dip your finger in a small bowl of water and rub it around the edges of the wrapper. This will help the wrapper seal closed when you press the edges together.

▶ Spoon 1–2 teaspoons of the pumpkin mixture into the center of each wrapper. Close the press and pinch the edges together to seal the ravioli.

▶ If you are using your hands, fold the ravioli in half with your hands, and use a fork to press the edges together and make a pretty pattern.

▶ Place your prepared ravioli on a baking sheet lined with a Silpat or parchment paper until you are ready to cook them. If it will be longer than 30 minutes, cover them and place them in the refrigerator.

▶ Use a slotted spoon to place the ravioli in a large saucepan of simmering chicken broth and simmer for about 7 minutes.

▶ Meanwhile, rinse and dry the parsley. Pick the leaves from the stem. Save the stem for your compost or your chickens.

▶ Spoon the ravioli into bowls and drizzle with olive oil.

▶ Add more Parmesan if desired.

▶ Sprinkle with parsley and enjoy!

# Miso-Glazed Salmon

**Serves 4**

Although salmon live in the ocean, they rely on habitat management to keep the rivers where they spawn pristine. Alaska's rivers are largely undisturbed and haven't faced logging and damming challenges like those in California and Oregon. For this reason, at the time of this book's printing, the Monterey Bay Aquarium ranks wild-caught Alaskan salmon as a "Best Choice."

☐ ¼ cup sake or dry sherry

☐ ¼ cup miso, light yellow, or alternatively white or red

☐ ¼ cup mirin (sweet Japanese rice wine)

☐ 2 tablespoons soy sauce

☐ 2 tablespoons brown sugar

☐ 4 salmon fillets, 6 ounces each

☐ 2 tablespoons canola oil (for the pan)

☐ Chopped basil for garnish

**2-3  4-6  7-10  11+**

▶ Measure the sake, miso, mirin, soy sauce, and brown sugar, and pour them into a baking dish (with sides).

▶ Stir the marinade, making sure that the sugar has dissolved.

▶ Add the salmon to the mixture. Wash your hands.

▶ Let the salmon sit for 5 minutes and then turn it over. Cover and refrigerate for 2 hours.

▶ Remove from the refrigerator and let it come to room temperature.

▶ Heat canola oil in a large skillet on medium-high heat and sear the salmon for 4 minutes per side, or until done.

▶ Transfer the salmon to serving plates and garnish with chopped basil.

# Crispy Tofu Triangles with Asian Dipping Sauce

**Serves 4–6**

Tofu is the artist's equivalent of a blank canvas. It is simple and can be the foundation of a masterpiece. In this recipe, tofu is transformed into a crispy and appealing finger food that can be dipped in sauce or eaten solo. These protein-packed morsels can be served with a plethora of side dishes including Purple Rice and Roasted Broccoli with Lemon (see Chapter 5).

☐ 2 packages extra-firm tofu, preferably organic

☐ 3 tablespoons canola oil

**Asian dipping sauce:**

☐ 2 tablespoons soy sauce

☐ 1 tablespoon sesame oil

☐ ½ tablespoon honey, agave nectar, or brown sugar

☐ 1 tablespoon rice vinegar

☐ 1 clove garlic

☐ Fresh chives, to taste

☐ Chile oil, an optional addition to the sauce

| 2–3 | 4–6 | 7–10 | 11+ |

▶ Open and drain the packages of tofu and cut tofu into slices approximately ⅓" thick.

▶ Cut the slices diagonally into triangles.

▶ Line a rimmed baking sheet with a clean dish towel.

▶ Place the tofu triangles onto the towel in a single layer.

▶ Place another towel over the top of the tofu slices and then top with another baking sheet.

▶ Put something heavy on the top baking sheet, so that it presses down evenly on the tofu slices inside (like a tofu sandwich in between baking-sheet pieces of "bread"!).

▶ Allow the tofu to rest for 30 minutes to 1 hour. This will press the extra liquid out of the tofu and allow it to get crispy in the pan when cooked.

▶ Heat a heavy-bottomed skillet over medium-high heat and add the of canola oil.

▶ When the oil starts to shimmer, carefully place the tofu triangles into the pan.

▶ Cook the tofu approximately 2½–3 minutes on each side, or until golden brown and crisp.

▶ Remove from the skillet and drain on a plate lined with a clean dish towel, a brown paper bag, or paper towels. Pat the tops of the tofu slices to absorb the oil as well.

**To prepare Asian dipping sauce:**

▶ Measure the soy sauce, sesame oil, honey (or agave nectar/brown sugar), and rice vinegar, and pour into a small bowl. Stir to mix all of the ingredients together.

▶ Peel the paper skin off the garlic. Use a garlic press to mash the garlic, and add it to the sauce.

▶ Use clean scissors to snip some chives into the sauce, for color and a wonderful mild onion flavor.

## KID ZONE
### Slip and Slide

Since honey is sticky and difficult to get out of your measuring tools, measure the oil first. Then, using the same measuring device, measure the honey. The oil left in the measuring spoon will help the honey slip right into the sauce mixture without any scooping or swiping! What other ingredients can you measure with this slippery strategy?

# Turkey Toes

**Serves 4-6**

It's hard to deny that children love chicken nuggets. Sadly, though, most commercial chicken nuggets hardly contain any chicken! This recipe is the real thing and is the perfect recipe to demonstrate how important it is for kids to know what is really in their food. Gather the troops—this is an ideal recipe for lots of little hands.

- ☐ 2 eggs
- ☐ ¾ cup flour
- ☐ Pinch of salt
- ☐ 1½ cups bread crumbs, or 3–4 slices of day-old bread
- ☐ 1 pound ground turkey, mixed light and dark meat
- ☐ ½ teaspoon salt
- ☐ 2 teaspoons Parmesan cheese, grated
- ☐ 1 teaspoon fresh basil or parsley leaves, chopped
- ☐ ½ cup vegetable oil

**2-3** | 4-6 | **7-10** | **11+**

▶ Take out three shallow bowls and crack the eggs into one of them. Fish out any stray shells and beat the eggs gently.

▶ Measure the flour and add to the second bowl, along with a pinch of salt.

▶ Measure the bread crumbs, and add them to the third bowl.

▶ If you want to make your own bread crumbs, simply pulse the day-old bread in a food processor. If you only have fresh bread, you can toast the slices first.

▶ Put the ground turkey into a large bowl. Set the bowl on the counter on top of a damp cloth, so it doesn't slip. Add the salt, Parmesan cheese, and basil or parsley (if using) to the ground turkey.

▶ Put some flour on your hands, and then pick up a heaping tablespoon of ground turkey.

▶ Roll it in the palm of your hands to create a smooth ball, about the size of a Ping-Pong ball.

- Set the turkey ball on a cookie sheet. Continue until all of the turkey has been made into balls.

- Pick up each ball, roll it in the flour, dip it in the egg, and then roll in the bread crumbs.

- Gently press each ball with the palm of your hand to form the shape of your choice, and put back onto the cookie sheet.

- Heat a skillet with ¼ cup vegetable oil on medium-low heat until the oil shimmers.

- Place half of the turkey pieces into the skillet. After about 2–3 minutes, gently turn over to cook the other side for about 2 more minutes.

- Remove turkey pieces from the pan and set them on a paper grocery bag or clean dish towel to drain.

- Repeat with the remaining oil and turkey.

- Serve hot.

## ☑ RECIPE FOR ACTION
## Gleaning: Harvesting for Students

I am blessed to live in a region of the country where farmers can grow amazing produce all year. Marin Organic sets the gold standard for promoting local agriculture and encouraging partnerships between farms and schools. Instead of plowing under the 20 percent of produce that doesn't meet the market standard, Marin Organic has started a gleaning program. Volunteers gather at a designated farm each week to harvest all of the produce that would not otherwise make it to the marketplace. All of that food is packed up and delivered to over half of the schools in Marin County. Those schools, in return, have designated a small portion of their food budget to put back into additional produce from those farms. Money is going back into our local economies, and our children are eating locally grown organic produce. It is a win-win situation, for the farmers, the kids, the community, and the planet.

# Pretzel-Coated Chicken

**Serves 4-6**

Don't you hate it when you reach into your bag of pretzels and discover that there are only bits, pieces, and pretzel dust remaining? This is an ideal recipe to use up the leftovers at the bottom of your bag! What a way to love the planet—recycling ingredients!

- ☐ 2 boneless, skinless chicken breasts
- ☐ Several sprigs of fresh thyme
- ☐ 2 cups salted pretzel pieces and bits (preferably whole grain)
- ☐ Salt and pepper, to taste
- ☐ 1 egg
- ☐ Olive oil, for frying
- ☐ Lemon for serving, optional
- ☐ Yellow or brown mustard, optional

**2-3** 4-6 **7-10** **11+**

▶ Place each chicken breast between two slices of plastic wrap.

▶ Using a small skillet, pound the chicken until it is flat. Repeat with the remaining chicken breast. (If you don't want to pound the chicken, you can use breast tenderloins instead, but they aren't as much fun to prepare!)

▶ Pick the thyme leaves from the stem.

▶ Chop the thyme leaves finely.

- ▶ Place the pretzels in a food processor or blender and grind until fine.

- ▶ Or, if you have some extra energy to burn, you can smash the pretzels yourself! Put them in a zip-top bag, squeeze out the air, and zip the top. Then, roll a rolling pin back and forth over the bag, until the pretzels are mashed. If you are feeling really cranky, you can bash the bag with the back of a small skillet. But be careful not to smash fingers!

- ▶ Transfer the ground pretzels to a shallow dish. Add the thyme and some salt and pepper.

- ▶ Crack the egg into a separate bowl and fish out any stray shells. Add a splash of water to the egg, and beat it with a fork or whisk until well blended.

- ▶ Preheat a large nonstick skillet with ¼" of olive oil over medium-high heat.

- ▶ Sprinkle each chicken breast with salt and pepper. Dip each chicken breast in the egg, and then hold it over the egg bowl to drain off the extra liquid.

- ▶ Then, dip the chicken into the ground pretzels.

- ▶ Press the chicken into the pretzels to help them stick together. Turn the chicken over and coat the other side. Wash your hands.

- ▶ Add each pretzel-coated chicken breast to the hot oil.

- ▶ Be sure that the chicken is in a single layer in the skillet. If necessary, cook in two batches to avoid overcrowding. Cook each side for about 3–4 minutes, until the pretzel coating is evenly browned and the juices run clear when you pierce the meat. Once you remove the chicken from the skillet, slice into individual portions.

- ▶ Optional: Squeeze fresh lemon juice over each slice of chicken. Or, serve with mustard on the side, to mimic the flavors when you eat a giant soft pretzel!

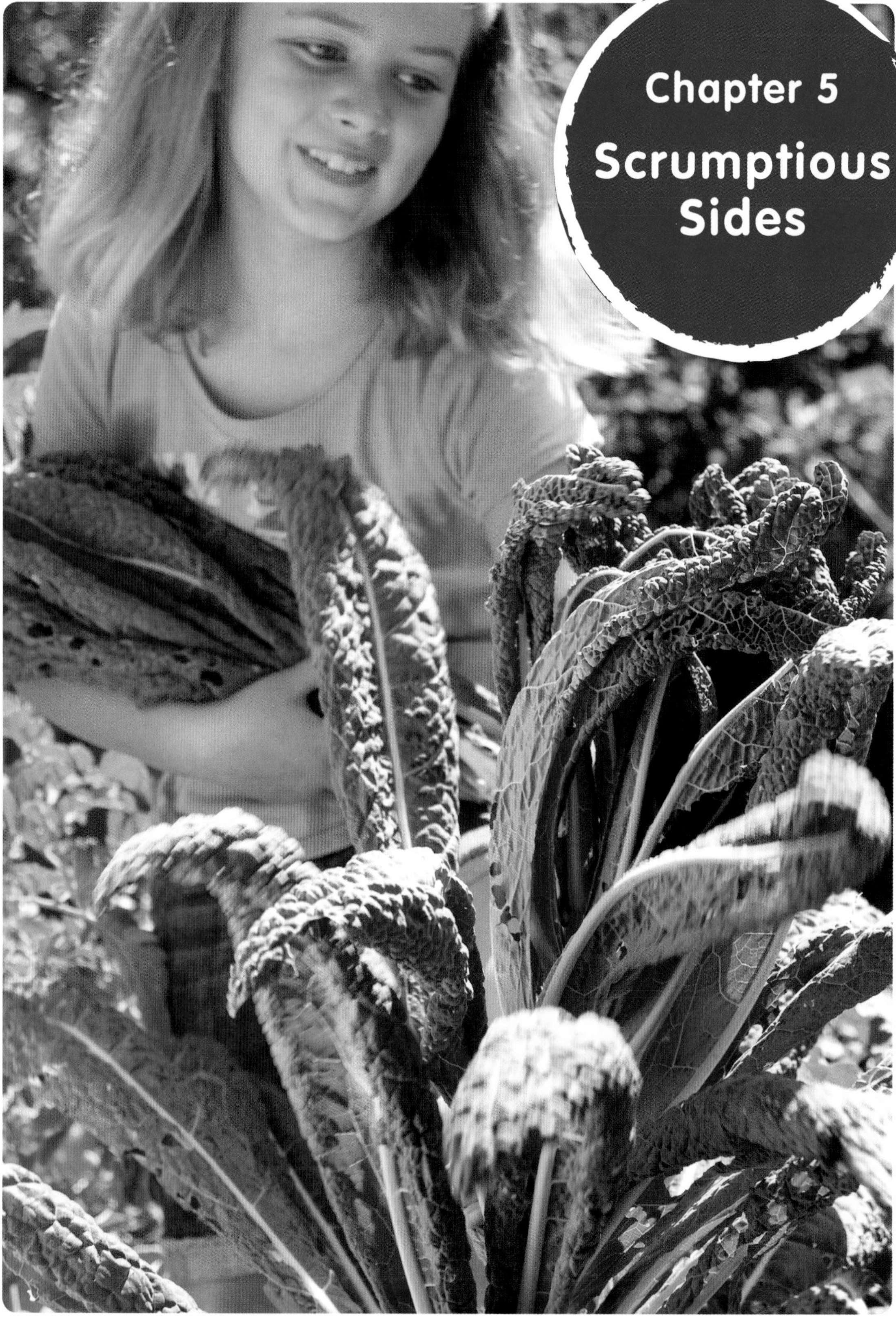

# Chapter 5
# Scrumptious Sides

# Kale Chips

**Makes 2 cups**

For people like me who tend to eat just a few too many tortilla chips, this recipe is pure heaven. It's hard to argue with eating too much kale! There are many varieties of kale, but our favorite for this recipe is dinosaur kale, which has thicker leaves that become perfectly crunchy when roasted.

- ☐ Bunch of dinosaur kale
- ☐ Olive oil
- ☐ Salt to taste

**2-3** 4-6 **7-10** **11+**

▶ Preheat oven to 350°F.

▶ Hold the thick end of the kale stem with one hand and run the pinched fingers of your other hand along the stem, stripping the leaf away. Tear the leaves into bite-size pieces or leave them in strips for larger chips.

▶ Brush both sides of each piece with a little bit of olive oil, or toss them with oil directly on your baking tray. With clean hands, sprinkle the kale with salt and toss again. Wash your oily hands when you are finished.

▶ Place the pieces of kale in a single layer on a cookie sheet.

▶ Bake for 12–14 minutes or until crisp.

▶ Keep an eye on them so they don't burn!

# Potato Latkes

**Serves 6**

Nothing quite says "Hanukkah" more than a plate full of hot and crispy potato latkes. I think it's time that everyone knows how to make these beauties. Tear open an old paper grocery bag and use that to absorb the oil from the latkes when they have finished cooking. This technique is more absorbent than paper towels, and allows you to reuse something you probably already have on hand instead of using something new. Potato latkes are delicious served with applesauce and sour cream.

- ☐ 1 pound russet potatoes, organic if possible
- ☐ 1 small yellow onion
- ☐ 3 tablespoons flour
- ☐ ½ teaspoon kosher salt
- ☐ 1 large egg
- ☐ ½–¾ cup canola oil

**2-3** | 4-6 | **7-10** | **11+**

▶ Preheat oven to 250°F.

▶ Peel the potatoes.

▶ Put the potatoes into the top of the food processor, fitted with the fine grating blade. After an adult or older sibling fits the lid on securely, pulse until each batch is grated. Repeat with the remaining potatoes.

▶ As you need more space in the food processor, transfer the grated potatoes into a large bowl of cold water to prevent them from turning brown.

▶ Add the onion to the food processor and grate.

▶ Once all of the potatoes and onion have been grated, drain them in a colander. Spread grated potatoes and onion on a kitchen towel.

▶ Roll up the towel and twist the ends tightly to wring out as much liquid as possible.

▶ Transfer grated potatoes and onion to a large mixing bowl. Measure the flour and salt, and stir them into the potatoes.

▶ In a separate small bowl, crack the egg, making sure to fish out any stray shells. Lightly beat the egg with a fork or whisk and pour it over the potato mixture.

▶ Stir to combine with a spoon or with clean hands.

▶ Heat ¼ cup oil in a 12" nonstick skillet over moderately high heat until hot.

▶ Working in small batches of four latkes at a time, scoop two tablespoons of the potato mixture into the skillet, flattening the pile gently with the back of the spoon.

▶ Reduce heat to medium and cook each side until the bottom of each latke is browned, about 5 minutes per side.

▶ Cut open a grocery bag and lay it on a large platter or the counter.

▶ Using a slotted spatula, remove the latkes from the oil and place them onto the brown paper bag to drain. Sprinkle with kosher salt.

▶ Add more oil to the skillet, as needed, and repeat with the remaining shredded potato mixture.

▶ Keep the latkes warm by placing them on a wire rack set on top of a baking sheet in the oven.

# Carrot-Raisin Salad

**Serves 6**

What's not to love about carrots? They are colorful, sweet, and crunchy. We sometimes take the carrot for granted—it is available all year long and usually gets eaten straight out of the refrigerator, without adornment. In this recipe, carrots get a makeover and are transformed into something that feels brand new. There are rumors from my recipe testers that their formerly non-carrot-loving children have been converted!

- ☐ 1 pound carrots (about 6 medium)
- ☐ 1 cup raisins
- ☐ 1 lemon
- ☐ 1–2 oranges, to taste
- ☐ ¼ cup light brown sugar
- ☐ Salt, to taste
- ☐ 2 tablespoons poppy seeds (available in the spice aisle)

| 2-3 | 4-6 | 7-10 | 11+ |

▶ Grate the carrots either with a rotary grater (to protect little fingers) or with the fine shredding blade on your food processor. Kids can load the carrots, put the lid on, and press the power button. We prefer the thin strips of the carrot from this method.

▶ Put the carrots in a serving bowl. Measure the raisins and add them to the carrots.

▶ Juice the lemon and orange into the carrots.

▶ Measure the brown sugar and add it to the carrots.

- Add the salt and poppy seeds to the salad, and stir to mix.

- Store in the refrigerator until you are ready to eat.

- As the salad sits, the raisins will plump a bit and the carrots will absorb more of the citrus flavor.

## GOING GREEN
## Down to Earth: Winter Gardening

Even if you live in an area where the ground beneath your feet is frozen solid, you don't have to ignore your garden during the winter months. Raised beds, hoop houses, and greenhouses can extend your growing season, and can even be helpful in other regions to protect tender shoots and lettuces. Or if it's too cold to tromp around in the garden, snuggle up with a few gardening books and seed catalogs and make plans for the spring.

If you are lucky enough to live in a warmer region, you can continue your vegetable garden during the winter. It's a great time to plant beets, carrots, parsnips, rutabagas, onions, kohlrabi, radish, lettuce, and spinach.

# Couscous Salad with Apricots, Ginger, and Pine Nuts

**Serves 6**

I'm always on the lookout for easy and delicious recipes to share at a potluck, and I couldn't help but notice this one when Mom served it at a party. It is one of my go-to recipes, especially when we are busy and time is of the essence.

- ☐ 1 cup whole wheat couscous
- ☐ ½ cup water
- ☐ 1¼ cups orange juice
- ☐ 2 tablespoons white wine vinegar
- ☐ ½ cup dried apricots

- ☐ 1" chunk of fresh gingerroot
- ☐ 2 tablespoons golden raisins
- ☐ 2 tablespoons pine nuts
- ☐ Salt to taste

| 2-3 | 4-6 | 7-10 | 11+ |

▶ Measure the dry couscous and pour it into a medium-sized mixing bowl.

▶ Measure the water, orange juice, and vinegar and pour them into a small saucepan.

▶ Bring the liquid to a boil.

▶ Meanwhile, cut the apricots into thin slices. Use a knife or clean scissors.

▶ Peel and grate the gingerroot.

▶ Add the apricots, grated ginger, and raisins to the orange juice mixture. Add salt to the mixture and stir.

▶ Pour the hot liquid and fruit over the dried couscous.

▶ Cover and let sit for 20 minutes.

▶ In the meantime, measure the pine nuts and put them in a small dry skillet.

▶ Turn on the heat to low and cook them until they become fragrant and begin to turn light brown. Stir them frequently so that they do not burn. Set them aside to cool.

▶ After the 20 minutes have passed, gently fluff the couscous with a fork.

▶ Refrigerate until ready to serve. Immediately before serving, add the toasted pine nuts and taste for seasoning. If needed, add more salt and another splash of vinegar to brighten the flavors.

# Roasted Asparagus

**Serves 6**

I love eating asparagus, especially roasted. But as soon as I use the restroom afterward, I catch a reminder of a genetics assignment that I used to do with my high school biology students. In much the same way that genetics determine whether or not your ear lobes are attached or "loose," they also dictate who can or cannot detect a certain odor in your urine after eating asparagus. Contrary to popular belief, asparagus causes the same scent for everyone, but only some people can detect it!

- ☐ 1½ pounds fresh asparagus, trimmed
- ☐ 3 tablespoons extra-virgin olive oil
- ☐ ½ teaspoon coarse salt

| 2-3 | 4-6 | 7-10 | 11+ |

▶ Preheat the oven to 425°F.

▶ Hold the head of one asparagus spear in one hand, and the end in your other hand.

▶ Bend the asparagus spear until the tough bottom portion snaps off. Lay this shorter spear on a cutting board next to the remaining spears. Use it as a guide so that you know where to cut the others. Or, simply break one at a time.

▶ Spread asparagus on a baking sheet in a single layer and drizzle with olive oil. Use your hands to toss and evenly coat the asparagus. Sprinkle with salt.

▶ Roast the asparagus in the upper third of the oven until the spears are tender and slightly caramelized on the edges (about 10–12 minutes).

# Lemon-Grilled Artichokes with Garlic Aioli

*Adapted with permission from my friend, Shaina Olmanson, writer at Food For My Family.*

**Serves 6**

Eating artichokes feels like going on a dinner-table adventure. Unless you have tried one before, you may feel uncertain of how to take apart this beautiful flower and eat it. Yes—it's a flower! Simply pull off one petal at a time, put the fleshy tip between your teeth, pull the petal away, and scrape off the pulp with your bottom teeth. As you peel the petals away, you will see a fuzzy "choke" (inedible) on top of the delicious "heart." Kids adore eating these petals, especially with this delicious sauce to dip them in!

**For the artichokes:**

- ☐ 1½ lemons
- ☐ 3 whole artichokes
- ☐ ¼ cup extra-virgin olive oil
- ☐ ½ teaspoon sea salt
- ☐ ½ teaspoon cracked black pepper
- ☐ 2 cloves garlic

**For the garlic aioli:**

- ☐ ¼ cup mayonnaise
- ☐ 2 cloves garlic, minced
- ☐ Juice of ½ lemon
- ☐ 1 scallion, diced (or ½ shallot)
- ☐ ½ teaspoon salt
- ☐ Cracked black pepper, to taste

2-3  **4-6**  **7-10**  11+

- ▶ Fill a large bowl with water.

- ▶ Squeeze the juice from one lemon into the bowl, saving the rind.

- ▶ Halve the artichokes and immediately submerge in the water. This will prevent them from browning.

- ▶ Bring a 5-quart pot of water to a boil and add in the squeezed lemon rind.

- ▶ Transfer the artichokes to the boiling water. Boil for 20 minutes, stirring occasionally.

- ▶ Heat grill on high.

- ▶ Empty the lemon water from the bowl. Use the same bowl for the next few steps.

- ▶ Squeeze the juice from ½ lemon into the bowl.

- Measure olive oil, salt, and pepper into the bowl.

- Peel the paper skin from 2 cloves of garlic.

- Mash them with a garlic press and add to the olive oil and lemon juice.

- When the artichokes are done boiling, drain them and toss them around in the bowl.

- Turn the grill down to a medium heat.

- Wearing protective BBQ mitts, use tongs to place artichokes on the grill.

- Baste the artichokes with the remaining oil and lemon mixture in the bowl.

- Turn every five minutes until artichokes start to char. Remove from heat.

**To prepare the aioli:**

- Mix together all ingredients in a small bowl.

- Serve with grilled artichokes.

- Dip the petals in the aioli, if desired, before eating.

## KID ZONE

# Worms: Good Recyclers and Inexpensive Pets

Worms? As pets? You'd be amazed at how much you will love them! They aren't very cuddly but they won't go potty in the house or chew on your favorite slippers. They will, however, devour all of your food scraps—and recycle them into the most amazing, nutrient-rich castings (a polite word for "poop.") Gardeners who don't like to use chemical fertilizers in their gardens refer to worm castings as "black gold" because it helps their plants grow so well!

Simply keep the worms in a covered box (with tiny air holes) lined with shredded newspaper. You can feed them coffee grounds every day, along with your banana peels and apple cores. Be careful—if your kids take good care of their worms, they may be looking for a pony next.

# Mediterranean Quinoa Salad

**Serves 4-6**

This salad is beautiful—the red quinoa provides the canvas, while specks of bright color flash throughout. If your family eats with their eyes first, they are likely to adore this meal. Plus, quinoa is packed with protein, so it is healthy too. (You don't have to mention that, though.)

- ☐ 6 cups unsalted water
- ☐ 1 cup red quinoa, rinsed until water is clear
- ☐ 1 cucumber
- ☐ 1 15-ounce can chickpeas/garbanzo beans (or ⅔ cup cooked dry beans)
- ☐ 1 cup cherry tomatoes
- ☐ 1 handful each fresh mint and basil
- ☐ 1 tablespoon fresh basil, chopped
- ☐ ½ cup kalamata olives, pitted
- ☐ 1 lemon
- ☐ ¼ cup olive oil
- ☐ ¼ teaspoon cumin or coriander
- ☐ 2 cloves garlic
- ☐ 4–6 green onions
- ☐ 1 handful parsley
- ☐ Salt, to taste
- ☐ Black pepper, to taste

**2-3** 4-6 **7-10** 11+

▶ Measure the water and pour it into a large pot.

▶ Bring water to a boil.

▶ Add quinoa to the boiling water and boil uncovered for 10–14 minutes. The little tails of each quinoa grain will pop out as they cook.

- ▶ Drain well and fluff with a fork after a few minutes.

- ▶ Peel the cucumber (if you prefer it that way).

- ▶ Cut the cucumber in half, lengthwise.

- ▶ Put the flat side down on the cutting board and cut into pieces, each about ½" in size.

- ▶ Open the can of garbanzo beans.

- ▶ Drain them in a colander over the sink and rinse thoroughly. (If you love garbanzo beans as much as I do, feel free to add the entire can to the recipe. Otherwise, measure out ⅔ cup.)

- ▶ Rinse the cherry tomatoes.

- ▶ Cut them in half.

- ▶ Pick the mint and basil leaves from the stem. Tear the leaves into tiny pieces.

- ▶ Slice the olives with an egg slicer or with a knife.

**For the dressing:**

- ▶ Cut the lemon in half.

- ▶ Use a reamer or juicer to juice the lemon (or squeeze it with your hands) and measure ¼ cup juice.

- ▶ Measure olive oil and combine in a bowl or jar with the lemon juice.

- ▶ Measure the cumin and add it to the oil and lemon dressing.

- ▶ Peel the papery skin from the garlic.

- ▶ Mince the garlic or mash it with a garlic press. Add it to the dressing.

- ▶ Snip the green onions into small pieces with kitchen scissors and add them to the dressing.

- ▶ Pick the parsley leaves from the stem and tear them into small pieces. Measure 1 cup and add to the dressing.

- ▶ Whisk the dressing or shake it in a lidded jar until well combined.

**To assemble:**

- ▶ Put all of the salad ingredients except salt and pepper into a large serving bowl and mix together. If you have a glass bowl, use it, so that you can see the bright colors of the ingredients. Toss with the dressing, to taste.

- ▶ Season with salt and pepper, to taste.

- ▶ Serve the salad warm or at room temperature.

# Oven-Fried Zucchini Sticks

**Serves 6**

It's hard to deny the appeal of finger foods. While the most common finger food on the dinner table may be the French fry, during the summer, you can easily replace it with these zucchini sticks. Serve them with a fresh tomato marinara sauce or even your child's favorite salad dressing.

- ☐ Canola or olive oil or cooking spray
- ☐ ½ cup whole wheat flour
- ☐ ½ cup all-purpose flour
- ☐ 2 tablespoons cornmeal
- ☐ 1½ teaspoons salt, plus more for sprinkling when the sticks come out of the oven
- ☐ ½ teaspoon freshly ground pepper
- ☐ Optional additions for the coating: paprika, dried herbs, cayenne pepper
- ☐ 1½ pounds zucchini (about 3 medium)
- ☐ 1 whole egg, or 2 egg whites

`2-3` `4-6` `7-10` `11+`

▶ Preheat oven to 475°F.

▶ Wipe a large baking sheet with a washcloth dipped in oil, or coat it with cooking spray.

▶ Measure flours, cornmeal, salt, and pepper.

▶ Pour the dry ingredients into a zip-top bag or a reusable plastic container with a lid. If you desire, you can add other flavorings to the coating, such as paprika, dried herbs, or a dash of cayenne pepper.

▶ Slice the zucchini in half, lengthwise.

▶ Place the flat side on your cutting surface and cut ½" slices down the length of each zucchini.

▶ If they are too long, cut the slices in half so they resemble French fries.

▶ Crack the egg over a small bowl and fish out any stray shells.

▶ Beat it lightly.

- Dip each piece of zucchini in the egg, holding the pieces over the bowl, to let the excess drip off.

- Put the zucchini sticks into the bag or container of coating mixture and seal it closed.

- Shake the container to coat the sticks in the mixture.

- Place a cooling rack over each baking sheet.

- Arrange the pieces of zucchini in a single layer on the cooling rack so that the hot air can circulate all around the sticks as they bake.

- Spray the zucchini sticks with cooking spray or brush each piece with oil.

- Bake on the center rack for 7 minutes.

- Using tongs, turn the zucchini pieces over and oil the other side.

- Continue to bake until golden and just tender, about 5–7 minutes more.

- Sprinkle with salt right after they come out of the oven. Serve hot.

## GOING GREEN
### Plan Ahead . . . and Save Gas

Thumb through the pages of your favorite magazines or cookbook (hopefully this one!) and write out a menu plan for the week. While you are at it, make a master grocery list. Not only will it save you the headache of last-minute shopping trips for forgotten items, this master list will actually save the planet. Well, not really. But it will make a difference in our air quality. If you make a shopping list for the whole week, you won't have to shop as often. Less time in the car means fewer climate-changing greenhouse gases and less air pollution. Oh yeah—it also saves you gas money!

# Israeli Couscous Salad with Summer Vegetables

 **Serves 6** It's fun to mix things up in the kitchen and try new ingredients. This recipe takes advantage of Israeli couscous pearls instead of the variety that you may be used to. This brightly flavored side dish was a favorite of my recipe testers. It pairs nicely with pan-seared pork chops, or a lighter fish dish.

- ☐ 1 small zucchini (approximately 4" long)
- ☐ 1 small yellow squash (approximately 4" long)
- ☐ 2 cups Israeli couscous
- ☐ 1 small red bell pepper, organic if possible
- ☐ 1 small orange bell pepper, organic if possible
- ☐ 1 lime
- ☐ 2 teaspoons curry powder
- ☐ 1 teaspoon cumin
- ☐ ½ teaspoon turmeric
- ☐ 2 teaspoons chili powder
- ☐ ¼ cup extra-virgin olive oil
- ☐ 3 tablespoons fresh flat leaf parsley
- ☐ Kosher salt and freshly ground black pepper, to taste

**2-3** | 4-6 | **7-10** | **11+**

▶ Bring a large pot of lightly salted water to a boil.

▶ Meanwhile, rinse the zucchini and yellow squash.

▶ To prevent these round squash from rolling around as you cut them, cut a thin slice from one of the sides. Then, place the squash with the flat side down on the cutting board.

▶ Cut ¼" slices from the zucchini and yellow squash, and then cut these slices crosswise to make ¼" cubes.

- ▶ Add the zucchini and yellow squash to the boiling water and cook just until tender but still crisp, about 2 minutes.

- ▶ Scoop the vegetables out of the water with a slotted spoon, reserving the boiling water. Rinse them under cold water and set them aside.

- ▶ Add the couscous to the boiling water and cook it until tender (as directed by the package, approximately 10 minutes).

- ▶ Drain the couscous in a colander over the sink.

- ▶ Rinse it well with cold running water, then drain it well again.

- ▶ Rinse the bell peppers.

- ▶ Dice the bell peppers and add them to the reserved squash.

- ▶ Juice the lime, measure out 2 tablespoons, and add the juice to a large bowl.

- ▶ Measure the curry powder, cumin, turmeric, and chili powder into the bowl, and stir. Measure the oil and whisk it into the lime juice mixture.

- ▶ Add the couscous, squash, bell peppers, and parsley to the large bowl.

- ▶ Toss with clean hands to combine.

- ▶ Season the mixture with salt and pepper.

- ▶ Cover and refrigerate before serving.

- ▶ If you prepare this salad a day or more ahead, you may need to add additional lime, salt, and pepper.

# Patriotic Fruit Salad

**Serves 4**

There is nothing like the first bite of fresh summer fruit—especially when you've waited more than eight months since your last serving. That's the blessing and the curse of eating seasonally. Sometimes it's hard to imagine waiting months to eat your favorite foods again, but there are huge benefits for the planet and your wallet if you're able to wait!

- ☐ 1 cup blueberries, organic if possible
- ☐ 1½ cups strawberries, organic if possible
- ☐ 3 white peaches, organic if possible
- ☐ 1 lemon
- ☐ 1 tablespoon honey or agave nectar

**2-3** **4-6** **7-10** **11+**

▶ Wash all of the fruit.

▶ Pour the blueberries into a large bowl.

▶ Cut the strawberries in half and add them to the blueberries.

▶ Cut the peaches into 1" pieces and add them to the other fruit.

▶ Zest the lemon with a zester or microplane. If using a zester, tear the zest strips into tiny pieces or chop them with a knife.

▶ Add the zest to the bowl.

▶ Slice the lemon in half.

▶ Squeeze the lemon and measure 2 tablespoons juice into the bowl.

▶ Measure and add honey or agave nectar to the fruit.

▶ Using a spatula or clean hands, toss fruit to combine the flavors.

▶ This salad tastes best when it has had at least 30 minutes for the flavors to meld.

▶ Store in the refrigerator and eat within two days. The peaches may discolor, but they still taste delicious.

# Spaghetti Squash Two Ways

**Serves 4**

Spaghetti squash is a dream for parents, especially those who are used to their kids refusing to try new foods. If your children love spaghetti, they will take comfort in the familiar shape of these squash strands.

☐ 1 spaghetti squash

**Optional toppings:**

☐ 3 tablespoons olive oil

☐ 3 tablespoons parsley

☐ ⅓ cup Parmesan cheese

**OR**

☐ 1 cup marinara sauce

☐ ¼ cup sliced kalamata olives

2-3 | 4-6 | 7-10 | 11+

▶ Cut squash in half lengthwise; remove seeds.

▶ Place squash cut sides up in a microwave dish with ¼ cup water.

▶ Cover with a damp towel and cook on high for 10–12 minutes, depending on the size of the squash. You should be able to easily pierce the squash with a fork when it is finished cooking.

▶ Or, you can bake the squash, cut side down on a baking dish in a 350°F oven for an hour, or until you can pierce the halves with a fork.

▶ Let cool for 5 minutes.

▶ Pull a fork lengthwise through the flesh to separate it into spaghetti-like strands.

**Options:**

▶ Toss the strands with olive oil, parsley, and Parmesan cheese.

▶ Or, you can top the squash with marinara sauce and sliced kalamata olives.

# Mashed Sweet Potatoes with Caramelized Apples

**Serves 4-6**

Nearly every family has a recipe that people beg for at holiday parties. This is the one that I am asked to bring to Thanksgiving every year! When I taught a group of preschool students to make this dish, one girl promised that she wouldn't like it. "I never like sweet potatoes," she said. But when her mom came to pick her up, the girl was on her third serving. Go figure.

- ☐ 4 medium sweet potatoes
- ☐ 1 cup whole milk
- ☐ 6 tablespoons butter
- ☐ 4 tablespoons light brown sugar

- ☐ Coarse salt and ground pepper, to taste
- ☐ 3 Macintosh or Gala apples
- ☐ 3 tablespoons butter
- ☐ 3 tablespoons brown sugar

**2-3** | **4-6** | **7-10** | **11+**

▶ Preheat the oven to 350°F.

▶ Rinse and peel the sweet potatoes.

▶ Cut them into 2" chunks.

▶ Set a steamer basket in a large saucepan.

▶ Fill the pan with enough water to come just below basket; bring to a boil, then reduce to a gentle simmer.

▶ Place sweet potatoes in steamer basket and cover; steam until tender, 15–25 minutes. Drain, and return to saucepan.

▶ While the sweet potatoes are steaming, measure milk, butter, and brown sugar, and pour them into a small saucepan.

▶ Bring them to a simmer, stirring occasionally.

▶ Once it has all melted together, remove the pan from the heat.

▶ Add the butter mixture to the drained sweet potatoes. Mash with a potato masher or with an immersion blender until smooth.

▶ Season with salt and pepper.

▶ Scoop the mashed sweet potatoes into a pretty baking dish.

**Prepare the caramelized apple topping:**

▶ If you have an apple peeler/corer/slicer, use it to peel and core the apples.

▶ If not, peel them with a vegetable peeler.

▶ Then, cut them in half lengthwise (from the stem to the base). Place them flat side down on the cutting board, so they won't wobble when you slice them.

▶ Slice into thin pieces.

▶ Melt 3 tablespoons butter in a large skillet over medium-high heat.

▶ Add apple slices and brown sugar.

▶ Cook for about 10 minutes, turning apples occasionally, until lightly browned on both sides. Place on top of sweet potatoes and bake 30 minutes, until heated through.

*Note:* You can make this dish ahead of time and store it covered in the refrigerator for a day or two until ready to use. If it has been in the refrigerator, allow an extra 15 minutes of baking time so that it heats through.

## GOING GREEN
## Your Face Is a Mess

Even though my conscience isn't bothered by the purchase of toilet paper, which is clearly a one-use item, I shy away from buying paper napkins. It's hard for me to justify spending money (and using environmental resources) for something we'll simply use to wipe off a watermelon-juice mustache and then throw away. Instead, in our house, we cut up old T-shirts and use them as napkins in lunch boxes and at the dinner table. When guests are over for dinner, or when we are feeling particularly fancy, we use matching cloth napkins (classy, right?).

If you find that paper products are necessary, try buying recycled-content paper goods. These use less energy to produce, and don't require any new trees to be chopped down (remember the Lorax?).

# Roasted Broccoli with Lemon

**Serves 4-6**

When I sat on the White House lawn as Michelle Obama talked about the Chefs Move to Schools initiative, she recalled some of her childhood food memories. She laughed as she told us about the mushy broccoli that her mother prepared, and compared it to the flavorful version that she now enjoys. By using a recipe like this one, you will be helping your children to develop a positive association with healthy food, and will be giving them a food memory they'll be unable to scoff at later!

- ☐ 2–3 stalks broccoli
- ☐ 1 tablespoon extra-virgin olive oil
- ☐ ¼ teaspoon salt, or to taste
- ☐ Freshly ground pepper
- ☐ Lemon wedges

**2-3**   4-6   **7-10**   **11+**

▶ Preheat oven to 450°F.

▶ Rinse the broccoli. Break the broccoli branches from the stalks.

▶ If the branches are too big, cut them into smaller pieces. Try to make the pieces approximately the same size so that they cook evenly.

▶ Peel the stalks with a vegetable peeler and cut them into chunks.

▶ Put the broccoli on a baking sheet.

▶ Measure the olive oil and pour onto the broccoli.

▶ Using clean hands, toss the broccoli with the oil.

▶ Sprinkle with salt and pepper, to taste, and toss again. Wash your hands.

▶ Put the tray into the oven and roast until the broccoli is tender and caramelized on the bottom, 10–12 minutes.

▶ Serve immediately, with lemon wedges.

# Green Salad with Pears, Walnuts, and Feta

 **Serves 4-6**

For years, I was against the idea of a salad spinner. It was just another object to store in my already-crowded kitchen cabinets. But after using one, I saw the light. It made such quick work of drying the lettuce that I never looked back. It has even earned a special parking space within easy reach inside my cabinet.

- ☐ 1–2 medium-sized ripe pears
- ☐ 2 tablespoons fresh lemon juice
- ☐ ½ cup coarsely chopped walnuts
- ☐ 1 small head lettuce
- ☐ ½ cup crumbled feta
- ☐ ¼ cup olive oil
- ☐ 3 tablespoons red wine, sherry, or champagne vinegar
- ☐ Black pepper, to taste (optional)

`2-3` `4-6` `7-10` `11+`

▶ Cut the pears into thin slices.

▶ Place them in a small bowl and drizzle with lemon juice to prevent them from turning brown.

▶ Heat a small skillet over medium heat.

▶ Add the walnuts to the pan, tossing frequently until fragrant. Remove from the heat.

▶ Wash and dry the lettuce. Break the lettuce into bite-sized pieces and put it in a medium-sized bowl.

▶ Add the walnuts to the lettuce.

▶ Measure the feta and crumble it with clean hands. Add it to the lettuce.

▶ Measure the olive oil. Drizzle the lettuce lightly with the olive oil. Measure the vinegar and pour it over the lettuce. Toss the salad with clean hands so that everything is evenly distributed and coated with dressing.

▶ If using, add black pepper, to taste.

▶ Serve the salad on individual plates and top with the slices of pears.

# Purple Rice

**Serves 6**

Purple rice? Talk about making an impression! Our group of cooking teachers was enthralled when our new member Mari shared this dish at our bimonthly meeting. It tastes like the sushi rice that my children adore, but has a fantastic purple appearance. My daughter thought that the color was from beets, but my son was worried that I may have added something "gross, like mashed bugs." Look at the ingredients for the recipe and see if you can guess where the purple comes from.

☐ 1½ cups short grain sushi or brown rice

☐ 2 tablespoons black rice (you can find this in the Asian section of the grocery store or in an Asian market)

☐ 1 teaspoon sesame oil

☐ 3 tablespoons seasoned rice vinegar

☐ ½ teaspoon salt

☐ 2 tablespoons sesame seeds

☐ ½ cup shelled and cooked edamame (optional)

☐ 1 sheet nori (seaweed), crumbled (in the Asian section of the grocery store or in an Asian market)

▶ Measure both types of rice and pour them into a colander.

▶ Rinse them thoroughly until the water is no longer cloudy.

▶ Add the rice to a pot or rice cooker.

▶ Measure the appropriate amount of water (as directed on the rice packages) and add to the pot.

▶ Let the rice sit in the water for an hour, without turning on the heat.

▶ After an hour, cook the rice until the water is absorbed, or until your rice cooker switches to the warming mode.

▶ Remove the rice from the pot or the rice cooker and pour into a serving bowl.

▶ Measure the sesame oil, seasoned rice vinegar, and salt, and add to the rice.

▶ Stir gently to combine.

▶ If you are using the edamame, add them to the rice. Sprinkle the sesame seeds on top of the rice before serving.

▶ If desired, top with crumbled pieces of nori (seaweed) right before serving.

## KID ZONE
### Eating a Rainbow

If you want to grow well and be healthy, doctors will tell you to "eat the colors of the rainbow" every day. That's pretty easy, especially if you eat lots of colorful fruits and veggies. The expression, of course, doesn't refer to foods that are colored by chemicals, such as Blue #1, Green #3, Red #40, or Yellow #5. Yep—you read that right. The Food and Drug Administration has approved a variety of chemicals to color our foods. The problem is that these colorants aren't made from real ingredients, and they make some kids feel pretty bad. The good news is that there are natural ways to add color to foods:

• Turmeric comes from the roots of an herb, and annatto comes from the seeds of a tree. Both of these extracts are bright yellow.
• Paprika comes from seed pods and makes foods turn bright orange.
• Red cabbage and beet juice turn foods red.

(In our Purple Rice recipe, the color comes from the black rice!)

# Step-on-the-Gas Baked Beans

**Serves 4-6**

Almost every time I make beans with my students or my own children, they launch into the catchy tune, "beans, beans, the musical fruit . . . ." You know the rest, I am sure. But you may not know what makes beans actually act as a "musical" food, causing not-so-fragrant bursts from the hineys of our otherwise respectful children. Have your kids check out the Kid Zone to learn about the science behind the action—and then ask them to tell you all about it!

- ☐ 2 cloves garlic
- ☐ 1 medium-size yellow onion
- ☐ 2 tablespoons olive oil
- ☐ 1 (15-ounce) can tomato sauce
- ☐ ½ cup light molasses (not blackstrap)
- ☐ 2 teaspoons mustard powder
- ☐ 1 teaspoon salt
- ☐ ¼ teaspoon ground allspice
- ☐ 1 bay leaf
- ☐ 2 (15-ounce) cans small white beans

`2-3`  `4-6`  `7-10`  `11+`

▶ Preheat the oven to 350°F.

▶ Peel the paper skin from the garlic and onion.

▶ Mash the garlic in a garlic press (or older children can help to chop the garlic finely.)

**Options for dicing the onion:**

▶ 1. Younger children can press the button on your food processor, if you don't mind the dirty dishes.

▶ 2. Or, if you have a safe food chopper, ask the kids to plunge the handle to chop the onion into teensy bits.

▶ 3. Older children can use a knife, with supervision.

- ▶ Preheat a medium-sized oven-safe pot over medium heat. Add the oil to the pot.

- ▶ Sauté the onions in the oil for about 10 minutes, until they are lightly browned (but not burned)

- ▶ Add the garlic and sauté for 1 more minute.

- ▶ Open the can of tomato sauce and add it to the pan.

- ▶ Add the molasses, mustard, salt, allspice, and bay leaf, and cook for about 5 minutes.

- ▶ Open the cans of beans.

- ▶ Pour the beans into a colander in the sink, and rinse.

- ▶ Add the beans to the pot, then cover the pot and transfer it to the oven. Bake for 1 hour. If you are really hungry, you can even skip this step—but it helps to deepen the flavors.

- ▶ Give the beans a stir just once, about 30 minutes into the baking process. The sauce will thicken as it cooks. Remove the bay leaf before serving. Serve hot!

## KID ZONE
# What Causes a Fart?

Don't let the stink discourage you—beans are an excellent source of protein, fiber, and many other nutrients. They simply contain sugar molecules that don't get broken down small enough to be digested. Our bodies don't have enzymes (chemicals that break down molecules) to break them into manageable-sized pieces. So the bacteria that live in your large intestines step in and chow down. Unfortunately for us, the bacteria releases gas as they break down their supper—and it escapes through the only opening available in your digestive tract. Yes, the one down there. Stop blaming the dog.

# Stick 'em Up: Frozen Choco Bananas

**Serves 6**

Chocolate-covered frozen bananas were one of my favorite desserts when I was a child. The frozen fruit takes on a creamy texture and the flavor is a perfect complement to the chocolate. Have fun with your toppings and turn this dessert into an edible craft!

- ☐ 2 bananas, firm but ripe
- ☐ 6 Popsicle sticks
- ☐ 1 cup water
- ☐ Optional toppings: coarsely chopped peanuts or toasted almonds, colorful sprinkles, toasted shredded coconut

- ☐ 1 cup semisweet chocolate chips
- ☐ 1½ teaspoons canola oil

**2-3**  4-6  **7-10**  **11+**

▶ Before starting, find a heatproof bowl that will nest over one of your saucepans. The steam from the simmering water will be your indirect heat source for melting the chocolate. Or, use a double-boiler, if you have one.

▶ Peel the bananas and cut them in thirds. Insert a stick in one end of each banana piece and set aside.

▶ Pour 1 cup of water into a saucepan, and turn the heat to high.

▶ Pour your desired toppings into several shallow bowls.

▶ Once the water begins to boil, reduce the heat to a simmer.

▶ Measure chocolate chips and canola oil and pour them into a heatproof bowl.

▶ Nest the bowl onto the saucepan over the simmering water. Stir the chocolate chips and oil until they are melted together and smooth.

▶ Line a baking sheet with a Silpat or unbleached parchment paper.

▶ Using a large serving spoon or a spatula, scoop up some of the melted chocolate.

*continued on next page*

**Stick 'em Up: Frozen Choco Bananas—continued**

▶ Roll one banana at a time, from side to side, in the melted chocolate on the spoon. Before the chocolate dries, sprinkle each banana with desired toppings. (To eliminate some of the mess, hold the chocolate-covered banana over the bowl of sprinkles as you scatter the toppings onto the wet chocolate. Don't dip the banana into the sprinkles because the chocolate will drip off the banana and will glop all over the sprinkles.)

▶ Set the finished bananas onto the prepared baking sheet.

▶ Place the bananas, still on the baking sheet, into the freezer for at least an hour before serving.

▶ Store the frozen bananas in an airtight bag or container in the freezer.

## NO TIME TO COMPROMISE
### Organic vs. Conventional

Bananas come with their own wrapper, which keeps out dirt and bugs, so you might think that because you peel this fruit, it doesn't matter if it's been sprayed with pesticides. On one hand, you're right—conventional bananas have been tested and reveal very little chemical contamination. However, you do still ingest small amounts of pesticides that enter the plant through its roots. In the grand scheme of things, though, if you are worried about toxins, bananas shouldn't be high on your worry-radar.

However, you may want to consider the ecosystem in which the bananas you purchase are grown. While conventional bananas might not pose a grave health threat to you, the pesticides used on them most likely have a negative impact on the other critters in the region. After all, the purpose of pesticides, herbicides, and other chemicals is to kill insects, weeds, and mold—not a great way to increase biodiversity in the area. Bottom line: If you can afford to buy organic bananas, the earth will thank you!

# Sweet and Crunchy Strawberry Cups

**Serves 8–10**

A delightful accompaniment to a warm summer day, this sweet, crispy dessert completes any meal. (Try not to substitute square wrappers for the round ones suggested. As the wonton cups bake, they get crispy, and the corners of square wrappers tend to poke the inside of your mouth—ouch!)

☐ 2 cups organic strawberries

☐ 4 tablespoons granulated sugar, divided use

☐ 24 round wonton wrappers

☐ 1 tablespoon butter, melted

☐ 1 cup heavy cream, organic if possible

☐ 1 tablespoon powdered sugar (confectioners' sugar)

| 2–3 | 4–6 | 7–10 | 11+ |
|-----|-----|------|-----|

### To prepare the fruit:

▶ Rinse the strawberries and pat dry.

▶ Remove the stems.

▶ Using a wire egg slicer or a knife, slice the strawberries.

▶ Pour 1–2 tablespoons of sugar over the berries, and let sit. They will become juicy.

### To make the wonton cups:

▶ Preheat oven to 375°F.

▶ Using your fingers or a tart shaper, press the wonton wrappers into the wells of a mini-muffin tray.

▶ Melt the butter.

▶ Using a pastry brush, paint the wonton wrappers with the melted butter. Sprinkle wrappers with remaining sugar.

▶ Place the tray in the oven.

▶ Check after 8 minutes. They are ready when they are golden brown.

▶ Remove from the oven and allow to cool on a cooling rack.

**To make the whipped cream:**

▶ Measure the cream and powdered sugar and pour into a medium-sized bowl.

▶ Using an electric hand mixer or immersion blender with a whisk attachment, beat the cream until stiff. It is ready when there are peaks in the cream when you lift up the beaters or whisk.

▶ Store the whipped cream in the refrigerator until ready to use.

**To assemble:**

▶ Using a slotted spoon, scoop some of the berries (without juice) into a small bowl. Scoop a few of these berries into the bottom of each wonton cup.

▶ Top with a dollop of whipped cream.

▶ Top the whipped cream with a few berries in juice.

▶ Enjoy, but be sure you have a napkin handy!

# Lemon Buttermilk Sherbet

*Thanks to my mom, Susan Stern, for contributing this delicious recipe to my book. It's the* Whole Family Cookbook *in every way.*

**Serves 4-6**

When you taste this sherbet, you will feel as if you ordered it from a fancy restaurant. No matter that there are only three ingredients! It goes to show that if you use quality products, you can create something good enough to land in a cookbook! Many thanks to my mom, who shared the bounty of her culinary experiments with my family, and turned me on to this recipe.

☐ 1 quart low-fat buttermilk

☐ 4 large lemons

☐ ½ cup sugar

| 2-3 | 4-6 | 7-10 | 11+ |

▶ Before starting this recipe, make sure that the bowl for your ice cream maker is frozen.

▶ Measure the buttermilk and pour into a medium-sized measuring bowl (ideally one with a pouring spout).

▶ Zest the lemons and cut the zest into small pieces with a knife.

▶ Cut the lemons in half.

▶ Juice the lemons and measure ½ cup juice. Be sure to pick out any stray seeds.

▶ Pour the lemon juice into the buttermilk.

▶ Measure sugar and add it to the lemon-buttermilk mixture.

▶ Refrigerate for approximately 15 minutes, or until the mixture is very cold and the sugar dissolves.

▶ Pour the cold mixture into the frozen bowl of an ice-cream maker and process for 20 minutes, or according to the manufacturer's directions. If you don't have an ice-cream maker, pour the mixture into a sturdy bowl or container and put it into the freezer.

▶ Remove from the freezer and stir vigorously every 45 minutes, for up to 3 hours.

▶ Add the lemon zest and continue for 10 more minutes.

▶ Store in an airtight container in the freezer for 2 weeks . . . although I doubt it will last that long!

# Simple Summer Frozen Yogurt

 **Serves 6–8** I love the idea of a light and refreshing serving of frozen yogurt, but was dismayed to find out that many stores sell a frozen product that is filled with lots of additives. This recipe is as pure as it gets. Made simply from yogurt, fruit, and sugar, it is easy on the wallet and the waistline!

☐ 2 cups summer fruit, such as peaches, nectarines, strawberries, mashed blueberries, or a combination

☐ ⅔ cup sugar

☐ 2 tablespoons lemon juice

☐ 1 (28-ounce) container plain low-fat yogurt or low-fat Greek-style yogurt, organic if possible

**2-3** **4-6** **7-10** **11+**

▶ Before starting this recipe, make sure that the bowl for your ice cream maker is frozen.

▶ Wash and slice the fruits of your choice, and place them in a bowl.

▶ Measure sugar and lemon juice and pour over fruit. Let the fruit sit for 10 minutes and then mash with a potato masher or purée with an immersion blender.

▶ Pour the plain yogurt and the fruit mixture into the frozen bowl of your ice-cream maker.

▶ Turn on and allow to chill for 25 minutes, or as long as directed by your machine's manufacturer. If you don't have an ice-cream maker, pour the mixture into a sturdy bowl or container and put it into the freezer. Remove from the freezer and stir vigorously every 45 minutes, for up to 3 hours.

▶ Serve the soft frozen yogurt immediately, or store in an airtight container in your freezer.

▶ If serving from the freezer, allow to sit for 10 minutes before scooping.

*Note:* Peaches and nectarines tend to be especially juicy. If these are the fruits you are using, reduce the quantity of yogurt by ⅓ cup so that it doesn't overflow from your machine.

# Peaches and Cream Cobbler

**Serves 8**

Every summer, my husband begs for a peaches and cream pie. This year, I am surprising him with a cobbler version, made from scratch. Check out your local farmer's market for an excellent selection of peaches. You just may have to taste them all before deciding on which ones to purchase. Bummer. Toward the end of the market, many farmers discount their produce so they can sell it off instead of transporting it back home. We scored our juicy organic peaches for just $1.50 a pound!

- ☐ 4 ounces cream cheese, softened
- ☐ 6 peaches, preferably organic
- ☐ ½ cup brown sugar
- ☐ 1 tablespoon cornstarch
- ☐ 1½ teaspoons cinnamon
- ☐ ¼ teaspoon ground nutmeg
- ☐ 1 egg
- ☐ 1 teaspoon pure vanilla extract
- ☐ 3 tablespoons brown sugar
- ☐ ⅓ cup sour cream

**Cobbler topping:**

- ☐ 1 cup all-purpose flour
- ☐ ½ cup whole wheat pastry flour or whole wheat flour
- ☐ ⅔ cup brown sugar
- ☐ 1 teaspoon baking powder
- ☐ ¼ teaspoon kosher salt
- ☐ 3 tablespoons melted butter
- ☐ 1 egg
- ☐ ½ cup milk

*continued on next page*

## Peaches and Cream Cobbler—continued

`2-3` `4-6` `7-10` `11+`

▶ Preheat oven to 425°F.

▶ Take the cream cheese out of the refrigerator before you gather the other ingredients. This should allow it to come to room temperature.

▶ Wash the peaches.

▶ Slice them or cut them into chunks.

▶ Coat the bottom of a 2-quart baking dish (or 8" Pyrex) with nonstick spray.

▶ Put the peach slices on the bottom of the baking dish.

▶ Measure brown sugar, cornstarch, cinnamon, and nutmeg and add to the peaches. Toss with clean hands.

▶ In a small bowl, crack 1 egg, fishing out any stray shells.

▶ Measure the vanilla and 3 tablespoons brown sugar and add it to the egg.

▶ If the cream cheese is soft to the touch, add it to the egg and vanilla. If it is still too cold and stiff, put it in the microwave on a microwave-safe dish and soften for 30 seconds.

▶ Measure the sour cream.

▶ Stir the sour cream, cream cheese, egg, vanilla, and brown sugar together.

▶ Spread the cream cheese mixture on top of the peaches.

**To prepare the cobbler topping:**

▶ Measure the flours, brown sugar, baking powder, and salt, and mix them together in a medium-sized bowl.

▶ Melt the butter.

▶ In a small bowl, crack the egg.

▶ Measure the milk, and add it to the egg.

▶ Add the melted butter to the milk and egg mixture. Stir to combine.

▶ Combine the wet and dry ingredients in the medium-sized bowl and stir gently to integrate the batter. It is okay if there are still a few lumps.

▶ Dollop the batter by spoonfuls over the top of the cream cheese mixture.

▶ In case the juices bubble over, put a rimmed baking sheet lined with foil on the rack below the baking dish.

▶ Bake for up to 25 minutes. Check after 15 minutes, and rotate the pan. The cobbler is done when the top is browned and cooked through. Allow to cool for at least 10 minutes before serving.

*Note:* Since you are baking this treat, remember that it's okay to use slightly bruised and ultra-ripe peaches. Taste them first to be sure they aren't fermented.

## KID ZONE
### How Do You Plant a
# Seedless Watermelon?

In order to grow seedless watermelon, farmers plant a special variety of seeds that would not produce any fruit if they were planted alone. Nearby, they plant another special variety of watermelon that produces pollen to fertilize the seedless watermelon plants. Lo and behold, the combination of the two different parents grows seedless watermelons. I spoke to several farmers who all said that growing these specialized fruits is pretty tricky. One farmer told me about a disaster that took place in his fields last year. By accident, only one variety of seeds was planted, and he ended up with a field filled with fruitless vines, and nothing to sell.

By the way—when we say "seedless" we are talking about the tough black seeds, not the flimsy white ones, which won't mature and can be easily digested if you swallow them with the fruit.

# Cinnamon Pear Clafouti

**Serves 4-6**

While a clafouti isn't much to look at, it takes just one bite to fall in love. First, you'll adore saying its name (kla-foo-tee)—try it, you'll see. It's as much fun to prepare as it is to say! Simply prepare the pudding in the blender and pour it over sweet seasonal fruits before baking. The resulting dish looks a bit like an inflated pancake, dotted with fresh fruit. Serve this rich and creamy treat warm, dusted with powdered sugar. (P.S. It makes a decadent breakfast, too!)

- ☐ 1 tablespoon unsalted butter
- ☐ 1¼ cups milk
- ☐ ⅓ cup sugar
- ☐ 2 teaspoons pure vanilla extract
- ☐ ⅛ teaspoon salt
- ☐ ½ cup unbleached all-purpose flour
- ☐ 3 eggs, at room temperature
- ☐ 1 lemon
- ☐ 3 Bartlett pears
- ☐ ¼ cup brown sugar
- ☐ 1 tablespoon cinnamon

**2-3  4-6  7-10  11+**

- ▶ Preheat oven to 350°F.

- ▶ Rub the butter along the insides of a shallow baking dish (8-cup capacity).

- ▶ Measure and pour the milk, sugar, vanilla, salt, and flour into a blender.

- ▶ Crack the eggs over a small bowl, checking for stray shells. Add the eggs to the blender.

- ▶ Rinse and dry the lemon.

- ▶ Zest the lemon and add the zest to the blender. Blend the batter mixture until it is light and fluffy.

- ▶ Peel the pears with a vegetable peeler.

- ▶ Cut the pears in half and scoop out the seeds with a small scoop or a melon baller. Slice the pears thinly.

- ▶ Lay the pear slices in a fan shape on the bottom of the baking dish.

- ▶ Measure the brown sugar and cinnamon and mix them together in a small bowl.

- ▶ Sprinkle the cinnamon/brown sugar over the pears.

- ▶ Pour the batter over the fruit.

- ▶ Bake until top is golden brown and custard is firm. Check after 35 minutes, and again every 5 minutes until a toothpick inserted into the center comes out clean.

# Apple Crisp with Vanilla Sauce

**Serves 8**

This crisp embodies the seasonal sweetness of a traditional pie but comes together more quickly. The decadent sauce, shared by my beloved great-aunt Beatte Berliner, makes this treat seem even more special. It's like you are serving a piece of fall on a plate.

**For the filling:**

☐ 8 apples, Pink Lady or Pippin

☐ 1 tablespoon sugar

☐ 1 teaspoon cinnamon

☐ 1 lemon

**For topping:**

☐ 1 cup flour

☐ ½ cup sugar

☐ 1 stick unsalted butter

**For the sauce:**

☐ 1 cup heavy cream

☐ 1 tablespoon powdered sugar, plus more for topping dessert

☐ ½ teaspoon vanilla

2-3　4-6　**7-10**　11+

▶ Preheat the oven to 350°F.

▶ Tip: Set up all of your ingredients ahead of time, but keep the butter in the refrigerator until you are ready to use it.

**For the filling:**

▶ Peel and core the apples. Save the peels and cores for your compost or your chickens.

▶ Cut the apples into 1–2" cubes or slice them (but not too thin).

▶ Put the apple pieces into a 9" x 13" ovenproof dish.

▶ Measure 1 tablespoon sugar and 1 teaspoon cinnamon, mix them together in a small bowl, and sprinkle the cinnamon sugar over the apples.

▶ Zest 1 lemon with a microplane grater or with a zester, and sprinkle the zest onto the apples.

▶ Toss the apple mixture with clean hands. Press it into the bottom of the baking dish.

**For the topping:**

▶ In a medium-sized bowl, mix the flour and sugar.

*continued on next page*

## Apple Crisp with Vanilla Sauce—continued

▶ Remove the butter from the refrigerator and cut it into small pieces.

▶ Add the butter to the flour mixture and quickly rub your hands through it, so that the butter becomes coated with the flour and sugar. You could also use a food processor to combine these ingredients, pulsing to create a crumbly texture.

▶ Crumble the topping over the apples.

▶ Bake for about 30–40 minutes, or until golden brown on top. Let sit for 15 minutes before serving.

**To prepare the sauce:**

▶ Measure the heavy cream and pour it into a medium-sized bowl.

▶ Whisk it until thickened but not stiff.

▶ Measure and add powdered sugar and vanilla. Gently stir to blend.

**To assemble:**

▶ Cover the bottom of each dessert plate with some sauce.

▶ Place one portion of apple crisp onto the sauce, and then top with powdered sugar.

*Note*: Feel free to use this formula with other fruits, such as peaches, nectarines, pears, or berries. You can also add slivered almonds to the topping for additional texture.

## GOING GREEN
### Living Pest Busters

Having chickens as a part of a farm or backyard ecosystem has its perks. They never tire of eating leftovers and kitchen scraps, and produce copious quantities of fertilizer and fresh eggs in return. Another benefit that may go unnoticed is their ability to find and consume insects. If there are pesky insects eating your crops, consider employing a few free-range chickens instead of using chemical pesticides.

# Chocolate Chip Pumpkin Bread

**Serves 8–10**

With the onset of fall comes a plethora of pumpkins. They serve as decorations set on windowsills, carved on porches, and scattered as centerpieces on dining room tables. What about in the kitchen? Guess what? The pumpkins you eat don't necessarily come in a can! This bread takes advantage of real pumpkins, which offers a special sweetness and seasonal flair.

- [ ] 2 cups unbleached all-purpose flour (or 1¼ cups unbleached all-purpose flour and ¾ cup whole wheat flour)
- [ ] 2 teaspoons baking powder
- [ ] ½ teaspoon baking soda
- [ ] 1 teaspoon salt
- [ ] 1 teaspoon ground cinnamon
- [ ] ⅛ teaspoon ground nutmeg

- [ ] 2 eggs
- [ ] 1 cup Puréed Pumpkin (see Chapter 7)
- [ ] 1 cup granulated sugar
- [ ] ½ cup light brown sugar, firmly packed
- [ ] ½ cup milk
- [ ] ¼ cup canola oil
- [ ] 2 cups semisweet chocolate chips

*continued on next page*

# Chocolate Chip Pumpkin Bread—continued

2-3  4-6  7-10  11+

▶ Preheat oven to 350°F.

▶ Measure flour, baking powder, baking soda, salt, and spices into a medium-sized bowl and mix until well blended.

▶ Crack eggs into a large bowl, fishing out any stray shells.

▶ Measure pumpkin, sugars, milk, and oil and pour into the large bowl.

▶ Beat the wet mixture until ingredients are well blended.

▶ Add the flour mixture to the wet ingredients, and stir until the dry ingredients become moist.

▶ Stir in the chocolate chips.

▶ Pour into greased 9" x 5" loaf pan.

▶ Bake for approximately 1 hour (or longer, depending on your oven temperature), or until toothpick inserted in center comes out clean.

▶ Cool for 10 minutes.

▶ Hold a plate against the top of the loaf pan and carefully turn them both over, so the loaf comes out of the pan and lands on the plate.

▶ Allow to cool completely before slicing.

# Coconut Macaroons

**Serves 12**

This recipe was born when I was teaching a preschool class at a Jewish preschool, and we needed something that was kosher for Passover. The kids were so smitten with the recipe that their parents started asking for the recipe, and now it is requested at every Passover party I attend! The recipe is so simple that your kids can do almost the entire process all by themselves, and the macaroons can be enjoyed year-round.

- ☐ 2 egg whites
- ☐ 14 ounces shredded coconut, sweetened or unsweetened, your preference (about 4½ cups)
- ☐ 1 (14-ounce) can sweetened condensed milk
- ☐ 1 teaspoon butter
- ☐ ¼ teaspoon salt
- ☐ Chocolate chips (optional)

| 2-3 | 4-6 | 7-10 | 11+ |

▶ Preheat the oven to 350°F.

▶ Crack one egg at a time over a large bowl. To separate the egg white from the yolk, carefully empty the cracked egg over an egg separator or clean hands—catching the yolk and letting the white drip through to the bowl below.

▶ You can save the yolks for another use in an airtight glass container in the refrigerator for up to four days, freeze in an ice cube tray (sprinkled with a pinch of sugar or salt, depending on how you plan to use them later), or discard them.

▶ Fish out any stray shells.

▶ Wash your hands when you are finished touching the eggs.

▶ Using an electric mixer, beat the egg whites until they are stiff. You will know they are done when the mixer leaves a pattern in the surface of the egg whites. Another clue that they are done comes when you lift up the beaters and they leave behind little peaks that look like the tips of chocolate chips.

▶ Measure the coconut and pour it into another large bowl.

▶ Open the can of condensed milk.

*continued on next page*

## Coconut Macaroons—continued

▶ Scoop the milk out of the can and into the coconut.

▶ Measure the butter.

▶ Melt the butter on the stove or in the microwave. Add the melted butter and salt to the coconut mixture.

▶ Stir the coconut mixture so all of the ingredients are blended together. It will be stiff, so it may take someone with muscles to help.

▶ Fold the egg whites into the coconut mixture until they are all combined.

▶ If you want to make chocolate macaroons, melt some chocolate chips and fold them into the mixture.

▶ Put a Silpat or sheet of unbleached parchment paper onto a baking sheet.

▶ Use an ice-cream scoop to scoop spoonfuls of the mixture onto your prepared baking sheet. (These cookies don't spread, so you can put them about 1" apart.)

▶ Bake for 25–30 minutes, or until golden brown. Cool the cookies on a rack before storing in an airtight container.

## KID ZONE
### What Does That Mean?
## Baking versus Roasting

You never hear about people roasting cookies or roasting a loaf of bread. But baking and roasting both involve cooking foods in the oven—so what's the difference?

Roasting is done in a shallow pan with some added fat or oil and usually results in a nice brown exterior, and a moist interior. It usually refers to meats and vegetables, and normally happens uncovered, so the food doesn't stew in its own juices. Baking usually occurs at lower temperatures than roasting, and often calls for the foods to be covered.

# Cherry Chocolate Chip Cookies

**Serves 12** This was one of the first cookie recipes that my nine-year-old daughter, Amelia, made almost all by herself. No wonder there were fewer dried cherries and chocolate chips than I expected—some of them never made it into the finished product!

- ☐ ⅓ cup whole wheat flour
- ☐ ⅓ cup all-purpose flour
- ☐ 1½ cups old-fashioned rolled oats
- ☐ ½ teaspoon salt
- ☐ 1 teaspoon baking soda
- ☐ 6 tablespoons unsalted butter
- ☐ ¾ cup brown sugar
- ☐ 1 egg
- ☐ 1 teaspoon vanilla
- ☐ ¾ cup dried cherries
- ☐ ¾ cup semisweet chocolate chips

| 2-3 | 4-6 | 7-10 | 11+ |

▶ Preheat the oven to 350°F.

▶ Measure flours, and scrape the excess flour from the top of the measuring cup with the back of a butter knife. Put flours into a large bowl.

▶ Add oats, salt, and baking soda to the large bowl with the flours. Stir gently with a whisk. If you are concerned about spills, nest this bowl inside an even larger one—that way, it's more likely that the spilled ingredients can be captured and reclaimed.

*continued on next page*

## Cherry Chocolate Chip Cookies—continued

▶ Melt the butter in a small saucepan or in a glass container in the microwave. Butter tends to splatter in the microwave, so cover it with a washcloth (unless you like to clean the ceiling of your microwave!).

▶ Remove the melted butter from the stove or microwave.

▶ Pour the brown sugar into the melted butter and stir until it forms a smooth mixture.

▶ Add the sugar mixture to the bowl with the dry ingredients.

▶ Beat with a mixer or hand mix with a spatula until well blended.

▶ Crack the egg into a small bowl. Pick out any stray shells. Beat the egg lightly.

▶ Add beaten egg, vanilla, cherries, and chocolate to the mixture in the large bowl, and mix until combined.

▶ Scoop out 1 tablespoon of dough at a time and place onto baking sheets coated lightly with cooking spray, 2" apart.

▶ Bake at 350°F for 12 minutes. Cool on the pans for a few minutes and then move them to cooling racks where they can rest until they are at room temperature.

▶ Store in an airtight container for up to a week. (Good luck with that!)

### GOING GREEN
### All Naturally Delicious?

Did you notice that these cookies contain whole grains and you can pronounce every ingredient? Plus, they don't come with unnecessary packaging. Now only if you could eat just one or two. . . .

# Flourless Chocolate Cake

*Many thanks to Daniela Weiner for permission to adapt this recipe.*

**Serves 12**

I tend to be an impulsive cook, simply gathering up all of my ingredients just after I decide to make a recipe. This lack of planning isn't very conducive to the requirement of many baking recipes for room-temperature eggs. If you are wondering, YES, the temperature of the eggs does matter. Cold eggs don't whip as well and can yield a denser dessert. Don't despair; you can still prepare tasty treats at the last minute. Simply put the cold eggs in a bowl of warm water for a few minutes, and that should do the trick. Alternately, you can put them in a bowl near the back of your stove as you preheat the oven below. Be forewarned—this cake is decadent and deserves to be shared with a large group of family and friends, along with a carafe of cold milk!

- ☐ 1 pound semisweet or bittersweet chocolate chips
- ☐ 1 cup light brown sugar
- ☐ ½ cup white sugar
- ☐ 1 teaspoon kosher salt
- ☐ ¾ cup prepared hot cocoa (see Chapter 7, or use any recipe that you like)
- ☐ 1 teaspoon pure vanilla extract
- ☐ 2 sticks unsalted butter, at room temperature (8 ounces)
- ☐ 8 eggs, at room temperature

**2-3** **4-6** **7-10** **11+**

▶ Preheat the oven to 350°F.

▶ Prepare a 10" springform pan by lining the bottom with parchment paper and thoroughly spraying the paper with nonstick spray (or rub with butter).

▶ Measure and pour the chocolate chips, brown and white sugars, and salt into the bowl of your food processor.

▶ Prepare your hot cocoa, making sure that it is HOT. Measure it along with the vanilla and pour them both into the dry mixture in the food processor.

▶ Blend them together until the chocolate melts and becomes liquid.

*continued on next page*

# Flourless Chocolate Cake—continued

▶ Add the butter to the food processor and blend until combined.

▶ Crack the eggs one at a time and add them to the mixture. Pulse together. The batter should be smooth and creamy.

▶ Scrape the batter into the prepared cake pan.

▶ Bake for 50–60 minutes. The cake should be puffed and have some cracks.

▶ Place the cake, still in the pan, on a wire rack and allow to cool. (If you pay attention, you will notice a gentle crackling sound as the air escapes from the cake and it begins to deflate! Don't worry—this is supposed to happen.)

▶ Cool the cake completely, release from the pan, and allow to rest in the refrigerator overnight. This cake tastes better the second day.

# Luscious Lemon Curd Tartlets

**Serves 8**

Most people probably associate lemon season with summer—it's hard not to think of lemonade stands on a hot day. But in our neck of the woods, Northern California, our lemon tree is happiest during the cool winter months, which is what inspired these delicious treats.

**Tartlet shells:**

☐ 1 package puff pastry, thawed

☐ 2 cups dried beans

☐ 18 mini-muffin papers

**Lemon curd:**

☐ 2 eggs

☐ ⅓ cup sugar

☐ 1 lemon

☐ ¼ cup unsalted butter

☐ Whipped cream, optional

**2-3  4-6  7-10  11+**

**To prepare tartlet shells:**

▶ Take the puff pastry out of the freezer and allow it to thaw on the kitchen counter (about 40 minutes).

▶ Preheat the oven to 400°F.

▶ There are usually two sheets of pastry in each package. Remove one from the package at a time.

▶ Unfold one of the puff pastry sheets. If there are cracks along the seams, pinch them back together.

▶ Roll out the dough slightly with a rolling pin.

▶ Use a pizza cutter to cut the dough into eighteen 3" squares.

▶ Gently press each piece of dough into the well of a mini-muffin pan.

▶ Prick the bottoms with a fork.

▶ Pour a small scoop of dry beans into each of the mini-muffin papers.

▶ Place a bean-filled muffin paper into each well of the pan, on top of the pastry. This will prevent the center of the shell from puffing up while baking.

*continued on next page*

# Luscious Lemon Curd Tartlets—continued

▶ Bake according to package directions, removing from the oven when the edges look puffed and golden brown.

▶ Remove the tray from the oven and carefully lift out the bean-filled muffin papers.

▶ Dump out the beans and save them for future baking projects. You can also save the muffin papers, or you can recycle them.

▶ Move the puff pastry cups to a cooling rack and allow to cool until you are ready to use them.

**To make the lemon curd:**

▶ Crack eggs, one at a time over a small glass bowl. Pick out any stray shells and wash your hands.

▶ Beat the eggs with a fork or a small whisk. Add the sugar and stir until it dissolves.

▶ Juice the lemon into the bowl with the eggs and sugar.

▶ Be sure to fish out any stray seeds that may fall in!

▶ Cut up the butter into tiny chunks and add it to the other ingredients.

▶ Add about 2–3" of water to a large skillet.

▶ Turn on the heat. Once the water in the pan starts to simmer, set the glass bowl filled with ingredients into the water. It will be like you are giving it a bath!

▶ Stir the mixture often and you will notice that after about 15 minutes, it will begin to thicken and coat the back of the spoon.

▶ Once this happens, you can remove the glass bowl from the heat and turn off the stove.

▶ Let the mixture cool.

▶ Use what you need to complete the tartlets and store the rest in a covered container in the refrigerator. (It tastes really good spread on a buttered piece of toast.)

**To assemble the tartlets:**

▶ Assemble these desserts right before serving.

▶ Scoop cooled lemon curd into each puff pastry cup.

▶ Top with a dollop of whipped cream, if desired.

## KID ZONE

# Having Fun with Invisible Ink

Did you know that you can write secret messages . . . using lemon juice? Here's how it's done:

| | |
|---|---|
| ½ lemon | Cotton swab |
| Saucer | White paper |
| Water | Lamp |
| Teaspoon | |

**1.** Squeeze the lemon juice into the saucer.

**2.** Add a few drops of water and mix well with the spoon.

**3.** Dip the cotton swab into the lemon juice. Then use it to write a message on ordinary white paper. When it dries, the writing will be invisible.

**4.** When you want to read the message, heat the paper by holding it near a light bulb.

**What Happens:** The words appear on the paper!

**Why?** The juice of lemons and other fruits contain compounds of carbon. These are nearly colorless when dissolved in water. But when they are heated, the carbon compounds break down and produce carbon, which is black.

# Nutella Lace Cookies

*Recipe adapted with permission from Lauren McMillan, Celiac Teen.*

I probably spend more time than I should on Twitter and Facebook. But when I meet people like Lauren, age seventeen, it's worth it. Her blog, Celiac Teen, (*www.celiacteen.com*) is well-written, beautifully photographed, and filled with delicious recipes that accommodate her dietary needs. She instantly reminded me of my favorite high school students from my days as a teacher. I am so proud of her success and felt that you should know about her, too. Although this recipe is gluten free, it's full of flavor, so you won't miss a thing.

☐ 1 cup Nutella (chocolate hazelnut spread)

☐ ⅓ cup sugar

☐ 1 large egg

**2–3** | 4–6 | **7–10** | **11+**

▶ Measure Nutella and sugar and pour them into a mixing bowl.

▶ Using an electric mixer, mix them together until completely incorporated.

▶ Crack the egg over a small bowl, and fish out any stray shells.

▶ Add the egg to the Nutella and sugar and beat until completely mixed.

▶ Let the mixture rest for an hour at room temperature.

▶ Preheat oven to 350°F and line cookie sheets with Silpats or parchment paper.

▶ Place half-tablespoons of the batter a few inches apart on your cookie sheet. They will spread and become very thin. You should get about 12 cookies per sheet.

▶ Bake for 7–11 minutes, until the centers have bubbled and look done.

▶ Let cool on the pan for 10–15 minutes, then remove and let cool completely.

*Note:* These cookies will be very flat and thin when they are finished. Don't worry—you didn't do anything wrong!

# Butter

**Makes ½ cup**

Not only does the end result of this recipe taste delicious, but it teaches kids that food comes from real ingredients, and doesn't just "come" wrapped in paper and packaged in a box. Did you know that fat and body tissues act like sponges for chemicals and toxins? Ick! That's what you sometimes get with prepackaged food. To feed your family in the healthiest way possible, try using organic dairy whenever you can.

- ☐ ½ cup heavy cream, preferably organic
- ☐ A small jar or container with a lid that seals well (a leftover jam jar would do the trick)
- ☐ Salt and fresh herbs, such as chives or thyme, to taste (optional)

**2-3**　4-6　**7-10**　**11+**

▶ Wash and dry your container. Pour the cream into the container.

▶ Put the lid on nice and tight.

▶ Shake, shake, and shake some more.

▶ An alternative method that works well for a large group of kids is to wrap the container in a towel and put it inside a coffee can. Send the kids outside and have them kick it around awhile. (This is a win-win! You get a few moments of peace and quiet, the kids burn off some energy, and then you can all have a delish snack when they return!)

*continued on next page*

## Butter—continued

▶ At first, the cream will be whipped into whipped cream. As tempting as it might be, don't stop there. Keep on going and the whipped cream will begin to separate. The whitish liquid is sweet buttermilk, and the lumps at the bottom are butter!

▶ If you are adding herbs to your butter, stir them in before serving or storing the butter in the refrigerator. Now go and make some toast, pronto!

### KID ZONE
## No Whey!

Do you remember the fairy tale with Little Miss Muffet, who ate curds and whey? I always wondered what the heck they were talking about! When cheese is being made, whey is the liquid that is strained off after the milk solidifies into curds. It is much like the buttermilk that separates from the butter in this recipe!

# Pancake Mix

**Makes 6 cups\***

Although it is really easy to reach into the cabinet for a box of pancake mix, it's even easier to skip the trip to the store and make your own. Plus, it keeps you in control of the ingredients.

*\*6 cups of mix is enough to make 3 batches of pancakes*

- ☐ 4 cups all-purpose flour, unbleached
- ☐ 2 cups whole wheat flour
- ☐ 3 tablespoons baking powder
- ☐ 2 teaspoons kosher salt
- ☐ 3 tablespoons sugar

**To make pancakes:**

- ☐ 2 tablespoons butter
- ☐ 2 eggs
- ☐ 1½ cups low-fat milk
- ☐ 2 cups Pancake Mix (this page)

**2-3** **4-6** **7-10** **11+**

**To make the mix:**

▶ Measure all of the dry ingredients and pour them into an airtight container.

▶ Put the lid on.

▶ Shake the contents to combine.

▶ Use within the next three months.

**To use the mix and make pancakes:**

▶ Melt butter and set aside to cool.

▶ In a medium sized bowl, crack eggs. Fish out any stray shells. Gently beat the eggs.

▶ Measure the milk and add to the eggs.

▶ Shake the pancake mix so that all of the ingredients are spread equally throughout the mixture.

▶ Measure homemade pancake mix and add to the milk and eggs.

▶ Add the cooled melted butter to the batter.

▶ Stir to combine all of the ingredients together. It's okay if there are a few lumps.

▶ Cook in a skillet. Top with fresh fruit, cinnamon, powdered sugar, jam, or pure maple syrup.

# Fresh Basil Pesto

**Makes ³/₄ cup**

Why buy pesto, especially when you can whip it up in a snap, using a variety of ingredients that you have on hand? Use this recipe as a guide, but feel free to mix things up a bit. Have your kids make suggestions for other ingredients to add. You can put several options on the counter and let them be the executive chefs and make the final decisions. Try walnuts, different types of cheese, or spinach or sorrel leaves. The kids can also go into the garden to harvest the herbs—this step will give them even more ownership of the process and make them feel proud. One thing is for sure—pesto brightens up any dish. It also freezes well, so you can get a tasty reminder of summer even on the darkest days of winter.

- ☐ 2 bunches of basil or 4 large handfuls from your garden (about 3 cups total)
- ☐ ¼ cup pine nuts
- ☐ 2 garlic cloves
- ☐ ½–¾ cup extra-virgin olive oil
- ☐ ½ cup Parmigiano-Reggiano grated
- ☐ Salt and pepper, to taste

| 2-3 | 4-6 | **7-10** | 11+ |

▶ Wash and dry the basil.

▶ Pick the basil leaves from the stems. Save the stems for your chickens or your compost.

▶ Measure the basil leaves (pack them into the measuring cup) and pine nuts and add them to the bowl of a food processor.

▶ Peel the paper skin from the garlic cloves and add them to the basil.

- ▶ Pulse the ingredients in the food processor several times.

- ▶ Measure the olive oil.

- ▶ With the food processor running, slowly add the olive oil in a constant stream.

- ▶ Turn off the food processor and remove the lid. Scrape down the sides of the bowl with a flexible spatula, and push the ingredients back toward the blade. Put the lid back on and pulse again a few times.

- ▶ If you plan to freeze the pesto: Scoop it out now and pour it into the wells of an ice cube tray. Cover the tray and place in the freezer. When the pesto cubes are frozen, pop them out and store them in a freezer safe bag or container until ready to use. Add the cheese, salt, and pepper after the pesto cubes thaw.

- ▶ If you plan to use the pesto now: Grate the cheese, measure out ½ cup, add the grated cheese to the food processor, and pulse again.

- ▶ Add salt and pepper to taste.

## GOING GREEN
# Garnish with Edible Flowers

Usually when my herbs start to flower, I get a sinking feeling in my stomach with the realization that they are probably past their prime. This summer, though, I picked a generous handful of basil flowers along with the remaining leaves on the sad-looking stalk, and sautéed them together for a pasta dish. Not only did they add a beautiful touch to the plate, but they tasted delicious. Since then, I have been more eager to use edible flowers in other recipes. They add a burst of color and flavor to salads and look beautiful on cakes, too.

Give these edible petals a try: nasturtium, sugar snap pea, evening primrose, thistle, violet, rose, pansy, English daisy, borage, marigold, lemon/orange, and flowers from culinary herbs (mint, basil, oregano, chives, rocket/arugula, chamomile, dill, sage). Use flowers that you have grown yourself or ones that were grown with the intention of ending up in the kitchen. Garden centers and florists often use chemical or untreated manure fertilizers that are not intended for human consumption.

# Hummus

**Makes 1½ cups**

Hummus is a delicious and nutritious snack and is very easy to make at home. You can even make it on the cheap by substituting 2 cups dried beans, which can be used after soaking overnight and then boiling in fresh water until tender. If you like a spicier hummus, add a pinch of cayenne pepper, or try a little cumin.

- ☐ 2 cloves garlic
- ☐ 1 lemon
- ☐ 1 (16-ounce) can chickpeas (garbanzo beans)
- ☐ ¼ cup water
- ☐ ½ cup tahini
- ☐ 1 teaspoon sea salt or kosher salt

| 2-3 | 4-6 | **7-10** | **11+** |

▶ Peel the paper skin from the garlic.

▶ Cut open the lemon and juice it into a small bowl.

▶ Pick out the stray seeds and measure ¼ cup juice.

▶ Put the peeled garlic and the lemon juice in the blender or food processor.

▶ Open the can of beans and drain them in a colander in the sink.

▶ Pour them into the blender. Measure the water, tahini, and salt and add them to the other ingredients.

▶ Process the ingredients until smooth, scraping the sides occasionally.

*Note:* If you haven't gobbled up all of the fresh hummus, store the rest in an airtight container in the refrigerator for up to a week.

## KID ZONE
## Tasting What You Smell

Have you noticed that food doesn't taste good when you are sick and have a stubbed up node (stuffed up nose)? That's because your tongue is only able to recognize four types of flavors—sweet, sour, salt, and bitter. The rest of the wonderful flavors you associate with food come from your sense of smell. Scent molecules from the foods you are chewing travel up through the back of your throat and into your nose.

# Puréed Pumpkin

**Makes 2 cups**

At the farmers' market you may find special "pie pumpkins," which are smaller, sweeter, and smoother in texture than the one you usually purchase or harvest for Halloween. Pie pumpkins are about 8" in diameter and are available from September through the early part of December. If you wish to purchase one of these pumpkins specifically for cooking, look for one that is bright orange in color, firm, and has no bruises or soft spots. However, if you are eager to include the usual variety of pumpkin from your garden in your culinary festivities, you can easily do so! Simply add additional brown sugar or maple syrup to your recipe to compensate for its lack of sweetness.

☐ 1 4-pound pumpkin
☐ Nonstick vegetable spray

| 2-3 | 4-6 | 7-10 | 11+ |

▶ Preheat the oven to 350°F.

▶ Cut out the top of your pumpkin.

▶ Scoop out all seeds and strings.

▶ Slice the pumpkin vertically into 3"-wide strips.

▶ Place strips onto a baking sheet sprayed with nonstick spray.

▶ Bake in preheated oven for about 1 hour.

*continued on next page*

## GOING GREEN
## Saving Seeds

Pumpkin seeds can be used either to plant pumpkins next year, or roasted to eat this year! First, place them in a bowl of water and rub them between your hands. Then, pick out the orange pieces that are floating, and discard them. Drain the water and spread the seeds on a dish towel or paper towel to dry. Now they're ready to roast or to save for next year's garden. But if you do decide to plant them, know that they sprawl and vine, so be prepared for the pumpkins to take over!

## Puréed Pumpkin—continued

▶ When the strips are tender, remove them from the oven. Once they are cool enough to handle, scrape the pumpkin from the skins and put the pumpkin into a bowl. Save the skins for your chickens or your compost.

▶ Beat the pumpkin with an immersion blender or purée in a food processor until smooth.

▶ Use as directed in any recipe that calls for fresh puréed or canned pumpkin. It is also delicious in soups and homemade ice cream. You may freeze leftovers or store refrigerated in an airtight container for up to five days.

# Spice Rub Mix

**Makes ⅓ cup** We made a huge batch of this spice rub mix for our teachers this holiday season. My daughter poured batches of it into cute little jars, and tied a tiny demitasse spoon to each one with a ribbon.

☐ 1½ tablespoons brown sugar

☐ 1 tablespoon onion powder

☐ ½ tablespoon garlic salt

☐ 1½ tablespoons paprika

☐ 1 tablespoon cumin

☐ 1½ tablespoons chili powder

☐ ½ tablespoon coriander

| 2-3 | 4-6 | **7-10** | 11+ |

▶ Mix all of the ingredients together.

▶ Pour into jars, seal, and store out of direct sunlight for up to three months.

▶ If you attach a card to each jar, explain that this spice mixture can be rubbed onto fish, poultry, or meat before grilling.

# Hot Cocoa Mix

**Makes 2 cups**

People pay a premium for convenience. Who can blame them? But convenience often comes at a cost when it comes to foods. Take hot cocoa, for instance. When most people buy it, it comes in little envelopes and may be filled with mystery ingredients. The cost is high—you are paying for the packaging and for people to process your food. How about buying some quality ingredients, mixing them together, and storing them in a jar in your kitchen cabinet? It's convenient—all you have to do is scoop some into your warm milk (or coffee!). But it isn't costly for our planet. Plus, it makes a really cute gift, packaged in a reusable jar and tied with a colorful ribbon.

☐ ¾ cup sugar

☐ 2 cups unsweetened cocoa powder, Fair Trade if possible

☐ 1 cup mini semisweet chocolate chips or chopped chocolate, Fair Trade if possible

☐ Peppermint candies or candy canes, optional

**2-3** **4-6** **7-10** **11+**

**Make the dry mix:**

▶ Measure the sugar, cocoa powder, and chocolate chips, and pour them into a large bowl.

▶ If using, crush several peppermint candies or candy canes: Put them in the food processor and pulse a few times, OR put them inside a heavy zip-top bag and smash into pieces (not dust!) with the back of a small skillet or with a hammer.

▶ Add ¼ cup crushed peppermint candies to the chocolate mixture. Stir the ingredients together to combine.

*continued on next page*

## Hot Cocoa Mix—continued

▶ Store in an airtight container and use within three months.

▶ If you are giving this as a gift, divide evenly among several small jars and tie on a fancy ribbon. Make a gift tag that reads:

*Pour ¾ cup milk into a small saucepan. Whisk in ¼ cup cocoa mix, and bring to a low simmer. Serves 1.*

**To use the mix for hot cocoa:**

▶ Measure ¾ cup milk and pour it into a small saucepan.

▶ Turn on the heat to low and heat the milk slowly.

▶ Measure ¼ cup cocoa mix and whisk it into the hot milk. Serves 1.

## NO TIME TO COMPROMISE
### Fair Trade

Maybe you have developed a better shopping system than I have, but some days I can barely get through the aisles of the market with my kids. List in hand, I quickly move through the store and try to escape as quickly as possible. During times like this, I don't often pay enough attention to details. But here is one that I do look for—it's a label that says, "Fair Trade Certified," and it's usually on my coffee and chocolate. That label tells me that the people who have grown and processed these items have been paid and treated fairly. Fair Trade standards were developed to ensure human rights and environmental sustainability from the producer all the way to your plate. Come to think of it, I'll show the label to my kids and have them go on a scavenger hunt the next time we are shopping—that should keep them busy and make the experience a little less stressful!

# Appendix

# Tips for Teachers—
# Cooking in the Classroom

The kitchen is an ideal place to reinforce what our children are learning in school. Measuring, estimating, and counting reinforce math skills and make them relevant, especially to children who learn best by "doing." Predicting, observing, and causing changes in food are the fodder of scientific learning. Tasting and preparing foods from around the globe are an ideal way to learn about other cultures. And cooking with healthy and seasonal ingredients models healthy eating, which we certainly need to reinforce more and more in our growing country (and by growing, I mean in girth!).

Some of the following tips may be obvious to you, but they are worth mentioning for the safety and health of our students.

## Cleanliness

- Before starting any cooking activity with your students, model good hand-washing techniques. Be sure to show the children how you wash not only your palms, but also between your fingers, and the backs of your hands. It's also good to show them how to "scritch-scratch" the soap on your palms with the tips of your fingers to clean under your fingernails. Who knows what has been gathering under there. . . .

- If you have long hair, tie it back. Nobody likes strands of hair in their food.

- If anyone touches his face or hair or teeth, gently remind him to wash his hands again. Younger kids need frequent reminding since they seem to adore scratching the insides of their noses!

- Have clean and dry dish towels and dish soap at the ready.

- Have two scrubbies handy—one for washing dishes with soap; the other for scrubbing vegetables (be sure to keep this one soap-free!).

## Safety

- Have two clean and DRY potholders in a convenient location.

- Depending on the age of your students, you might want to use blue painter's tape to make a "safety zone" around an electric skillet, burner, oven, or stove. Students should stay on the outside of the taped area unless they are supervised by an adult and are actively stirring the cooking food.

- If you are using knives in your class, be sure to wash them immediately after use and return them to their safe storage location. Knives can easily get lost under soapy water in the sink and can cut unsuspecting dishwashers.

- Always carry knives at your side with the tip pointing toward the floor.

- Before cutting rounded objects, such as potatoes, carrots, or zucchini, give the food a flat edge so that the food doesn't roll around on the cutting board. Do this by cutting a small slice from one side of the food so that it can lie flat on your work surface.

## Teaching

- Try to include every student—this may mean giving each student a small task. Tasks can include reading the recipe aloud, checking to be sure that you have included all of the ingredients, washing produce or dishes, drying dishes, measuring or stirring, or helping another student.

- Encourage all of the students to taste the food. If they are hesitant, don't force them, but enthusiastically remind them that their own food tastes especially good. If they are fairly certain that they won't like the food, encourage them to take a "No, thank you" bite. Remember that forcing the issue can lead to issues about food later in life—and we want food to be associated with positive memories.

- Because students are easily influenced by their peers, ask them not to "yuk my yum," which loosely translates to "if you don't have something nice to say, don't say anything at all."

# Seasonal Recipe Index

## Winter

A-B-C (Apple Bacon Cheddar) Frittata. . . . . . . . . . . . . . . . . . 40

Biscuit-Topped Chicken Potpie. . . 79

Carrot-Raisin Salad. . . . . . . . . . . 114

Couscous Salad with Apricots, Ginger, and Pine Nuts . . . . . . . . . 116

Chicken Picatta with Linguine . . . . 68

Grandma's Spaghetti Gravy . . . . . 77

Kale Chips. . . . . . . . . . . . . . . . . 111

Luscious Lemon Curd Tartlets . . . . . . . . . . . . . . . . 158

Minestrone with White Beans and Kale . . . . . . . . . . . . . . . . . . . . 71

Mini Frittatas . . . . . . . . . . . . . . . . 14

Pork Ribs with Asian BBQ Sauce. . . 74

Potato Latkes . . . . . . . . . . . . . . . 112

Squashed Sweet Potato Soup . . . 45

Wrap It Up: BBQ Style. . . . . . . . . 44

## Spring

Breakfast Anytime Pizza . . . . . . . . 15

Lemon Buttermilk Sherbet . . . . . . 142

Lemon-Grilled Artichokes with Garlic Aioli. . . . . . . . . . . . . . . . . . 118

Pork Chops with Sage Butter . . . . 84

Roasted Asparagus . . . . . . . . . . 117

Sorrel-icious Sole . . . . . . . . . . . . 86

Sweet and Crunchy Strawberry Cups. . . . . . . . . . . . . 139

Thai Spring Rolls. . . . . . . . . . . . . 49

Wish-for-a-Fish Pasta . . . . . . . . . 82

Wrap It Up: L'egg-o Style. . . . . . . 48

## Summer

Banana Sunshine Smoothie . . . . . 20

Corny Raspberry Muffins . . . . . . . 22

Fresh Basil Pesto . . . . . . . . . . . . 166

Israeli Couscous Salad with Summer Vegetables . . . . . . . . . . . 124

Mediterranean Quinoa Salad. . . . . 120

Oven-Fried Zucchini Sticks . . . . . . 122

Patriotic Fruit Salad. . . . . . . . . . . 126

Peaches and Cream Cobbler . . . . 144

Simple Summer Frozen Yogurt . . . 143

Smashed Avocado on Toast . . . . . 52

Yummy Strawberry Yogurt Parfait . . . . . . . . . . . . . . . 18

## Fall

Acorn Squash and Wild Rice Bowls . . . . . . . . . . . . . 96

Apple Crisp with Vanilla Sauce . . . 148

Baked Apple Puff . . . . . . . . . . . . 24

Chinese Chicken Salad. . . . . . . . . 53

Chocolate Chip Pumpkin Bread . . 150

Cinnamon Pear Clafouti . . . . . . . 147

Falling for Fall Quesadillas . . . . . . 98

Green Salad with Pears, Walnuts, and Feta . . . . . . . . . . . . 131

Mashed Sweet Potatoes with Caramelized Apples . . . . . . . . . . 128

Pumpkin Ravioli . . . . . . . . . . . . . 101

Puréed Pumpkin . . . . . . . . . . . . 169

R & B Chili . . . . . . . . . . . . . . . . . 56

Roasted Broccoli with Lemon . . . . 130

Spaghetti Squash Two Ways. . . . . 127

Steel-Cut Oatmeal with Dates. . . . 26

Sweet Potato Biscuits . . . . . . . . . 28

Taco Salad . . . . . . . . . . . . . . . . . 94

There's Turkey in My Pocket . . . . . 55

Wrap It Up: Toga Style. . . . . . . . . 60

## Any Season

Breakfast Burrito. . . . . . . . . . . . . 30

Butter . . . . . . . . . . . . . . . . . . . . 163

Cherry Chocolate Chip Cookies . . 154

Chewy Maple Granola Bars . . . . . 61

Coconut Macaroons . . . . . . . . . . 152

Crispy Tofu Triangles with Asian Dipping Sauce . . . . . . . . . . . . . . 104

Croque Monsieur . . . . . . . . . . . . 58

Crunchy Granola. . . . . . . . . . . . . 37

Flourless Chocolate Cake . . . . . . . 156

Grilled Cheese with Nutella . . . . . . 35

Hot Cocoa Mix . . . . . . . . . . . . . . 171

Hummus. . . . . . . . . . . . . . . . . . . 168

Miso-Glazed Salmon. . . . . . . . . . 103

Nutella Lace Cookies . . . . . . . . . . 161

Pancake Mix . . . . . . . . . . . . . . . 165

Pretzel-Coated Chicken . . . . . . . . 108

Purple Rice . . . . . . . . . . . . . . . . 132

Salty Pretzel Pillows . . . . . . . . . . 63

Spice Rub Mix. . . . . . . . . . . . . . . 170

Step-on-the-Gas Baked Beans. . . 134

Stick 'em Up: Frozen Choco Bananas . . . . . . . . . . . . . 137

Sweet and Salty Glazed Bacon. . . 21

Turkey Toes. . . . . . . . . . . . . . . . 106

# Index

## A

A-B-C Frittata, 40–41
Acorn Squash and Wild Rice Bowls, 96–97
Age appropriateness, of recipes, 8
Apples
    A-B-C Frittata, 40–41
    about: peeler/corer/slicer, 6
    Apple Crisp with Vanilla Sauce, 148–49
    Baked Apple Puff, 24–25
    Mashed Sweet Potatoes with Caramelized Apples, 128–29
Appliances, unplugging, 25
Artichokes, Lemon-Grilled with Garlic Aioli, 118–19
Asian Dipping Sauces, 104–5
Asparagus, Roasted, 117
Avocado
    about: as fruit or vegetable, 52
    Smashed Avocado on Toast, 52

## B

Baked Apple Puff, 24–25
Baking vs. roasting, 153
Bananas
    about: organic, pesticides and, 138
    Banana Sunshine Smoothie, 20
    Stick 'em Up: Frozen Choco Bananas, 159–60
Basil, in Fresh Basil Pesto, 166–67
Beans and legumes
    about: causes of farts and, 135; as fruits or vegetables, 52
    Breakfast Burrito, 30–32
    Hummus, 168
    Minestrone with White Beans and Kale, 71–72
    R & B Chili, 56–57
    Step-on-the-Gas Baked Beans, 134–35
    Taco Salad, 94–95
    Wrap It Up: Toga Style, 60
Beef
    about: pastured meat, 59
    Grandma's Spaghetti Gravy, 77–78
Bell peppers. See Peppers

Berries
    about: buying local, 23
    Corny Raspberry Muffins, 22–23
    Patriotic Fruit Salad, 126
    Simple Summer Frozen Yogurt, 144
    Sweet and Crunchy Strawberry Cups, 140–41
    Yummy Strawberry Yogurt Parfait, 18–19
Biscuit-Topped Chicken Potpie, 79–81
Blueberries. See Berries
Breads. See also Sandwiches and wraps
    about: mini-muffin tins, 6
    Chocolate Chip Pumpkin Bread, 150–51
    Corny Raspberry Muffins, 22–23
    Pancake Mix, 165
    Salty Pretzel Pillows, 63–66
    Smashed Avocado on Toast, 52
    Sweet Potato Biscuits, 28–29
Breakfast, 13–38
    Baked Apple Puff, 24–25
    Banana Sunshine Smoothie, 20
    Breakfast Anytime Pizza, 15–17
    Breakfast Burrito, 30–32
    Corny Raspberry Muffins, 22–23
    Crunchy Granola, 37–38
    Grilled Cheese with Nutella, 34, 35–36
    Mini Frittatas, 14
    Steel-Cut Oatmeal with Dates, 26–27
    Sweet and Salty Glazed Bacon, 21
    Sweet Potato Biscuits, 28–29
    Yummy Strawberry Yogurt Parfait, 18–19
Broccoli, Roasted, with Lemon, 130
Burritos
    about: helping hungry families with, 33
    Breakfast Burrito, 30–32
Butter, making, 163–64
Buttermilk, making, 164

## C

Cabbage, in Chinese Chicken Salad, 53–54

Canning foods, 4
Carrot-Raisin Salad, 114–15
Charity. See Helping others
Cheese
    about: buying local, 17; rotary grater for, 6
    A-B-C Frittata, 40–41
    Falling for Fall Quesadillas, 98–99
    Grilled Cheese with Nutella, 34, 35–36
    Pumpkin Ravioli, 101–2
    Wrap It Up: BBQ Style, 44
Cherry Chocolate Chip Cookies, 154–55
Chewy Maple Granola Bars, 61–62
Chicken
    Biscuit-Topped Chicken Potpie, 79–81
    Breakfast Burrito, 30–32
    Chicken Picatta with Linguine, 68–69
    Chinese Chicken Salad, 53–54
    Pretzel-Coated Chicken, 108–9
    sustainable farms and, 76
Chickens
    free-range and cage-free, 70
    pastured, 70
    raising, 43
    replacing pesticides, 149
Chickpeas. See Beans and legumes
Chinese Chicken Salad, 53–54
Chips, Kale, 111
Chocolate
    Cherry Chocolate Chip Cookies, 154–55
    Chocolate Chip Pumpkin Bread, 150–51
    Flourless Chocolate Cake, 156–57
    Grilled Cheese with Nutella, 34
    Hot Cocoa Mix, 171–73
    Nutella Lace Cookies, 161
    Stick 'em Up: Frozen Choco Bananas, 137–38
Choppers, 6
Cinnamon Pear Clafouti, 147
Cleanliness considerations, 175
Coconut Macaroons, 152–53
Colors of rainbow, eating, 133

Community Supported Agriculture
(CSA), 3
Composting, 47
Conserving resources, 60
Cookies
Cherry Chocolate Chip Cookies,
155–56
Coconut Macaroons, 152–53
Nutella Lace Cookies, 161
Cooking for a family in crisis, 78
Cooking with kids. *See* Kids in kitchen
Corny Raspberry Muffins, 22–23
Couscous
Couscous Salad with Apricots,
Ginger, and Pine Nuts, 116
Israeli Couscous Salad with
Summer Vegetables, 124–25
Cream, whipped, 141
Crispy Tofu Triangles with Asian
Dipping Sauce, 104–5
Croque Monsieur, 58
Crunchy Granola, 37–38
Cucumbers, as fruits or vegetables,
52

**D**

Dehydrating foods, 4
Desserts. *See* Treats
Dinner, 67–109
Acorn Squash and Wild Rice
Bowls, 96–97
Biscuit-Topped Chicken Potpie,
79–81
Chicken Picatta with Linguine,
68–69
Crispy Tofu Triangles with Asian
Dipping Sauce, 104–5
Falling for Fall Quesadillas, 98–99
Grandma's Spaghetti Gravy, 77–78
Greek Shrimp with Feta, 88–89
Minestrone with White Beans and
Kale, 71–72
Miso-Glazed Salmon, 103
Pork Chops with Sage Butter,
84–85
Pork Ribs with Asian BBQ Sauce,
74–75
Pretzel-Coated Chicken, 108–9
Pumpkin Ravioli, 101–2
Sorrel-icious Sole, 86–87
Summertime Kabobs with Udon
Noodles, 90–93
Taco Salad, 94–95

Turkey Toes, 106–7
Wish-for-a-Fish Pasta, 82
Drinks
Banana Sunshine Smoothie, 20
Hot Cocoa Mix, 171–73

**E**

Eating out, 4
Eggplant, as fruit or vegetable, 52
Eggs
about: free-range/cage-free
chickens and, 70; pastured
poultry and, 70; raising
chickens for, 43; understanding
package labels, 70
A-B-C Frittata, 40–41
Baked Apple Puff, 24–25
Breakfast Anytime Pizza, 15–17
Breakfast Burrito, 30–32
Mini Frittatas, 14
Wrap It Up: L'egg-o Style, 48
Environmental awareness issues. *See
also* Gardening
composting, 47
conserving resources, 60
Fair Trade Certified foods, 172
fishing techniques and tuna safety,
83
Great Pacific Garbage Patch, 38
Meatless Monday, 54
pastured meat, 59
pest control, 89, 149
planning shopping to save gas, 123
recyclable napkins, 129
sustainable farms, 76
unplugging unused appliances, 25

**F**

Fair Trade Certified foods, 172
Fall gardening, 99
Falling for Fall Quesadillas, 98–99
Farmer's market
buying foods at, 2, 23
locavores and. *See* Locavores
tasting samples at, 2
Farts, causes of, 135
Field trips, 4
Fish and seafood
about: tuna safety and fishing
techniques, 83
Greek Shrimp with Feta, 88–89
Miso-Glazed Salmon, 103

Sorrel-icious Sole, 86–87
Wish-for-a-Fish Pasta, 82
Flatulence, reasons for, 135
Flourless Chocolate Cake, 157–58
Flowers, edible, 167
Food choppers, 6
Freezing foods, 4
Fresh Basil Pesto, 166–67
Fruit. *See also* Berries; *specific fruit*
about: foods as vegetables or, 52;
requirement for foods to be, 52
Patriotic Fruit Salad, 126
Simple Summer Frozen Yogurt,
143

**G**

Gadgets/tools for kitchen, 6–7
Garbanzo beans. *See* Beans and
legumes
Gardening
composting and, 47
edible flowers, 167
fall, 99
greenhouses for, 115
growing seedless watermelons,
146
harvesting for students, 107
hoop houses for, 115
perennial edibles, 99
pest control, 89, 149
planting things, 3, 87, 89, 99, 115,
146
raised beds for, 115
saving pumpkin seeds for, 169
spring weeding/planting, 87
summer, 89
when to plant what, 87
winter, 115
worms and, 119
Garlic Aioli, 118–19
Garnishing with edible flowers, 167
Grains
Acorn Squash and Wild Rice
Bowls, 96–97
Cherry Chocolate Chip Cookies,
154–55
Chewy Maple Granola Bars,
61–62
Couscous Salad with Apricots,
Ginger, and Pine Nuts, 116
Crunchy Granola, 37–38
Israeli Couscous Salad with
Summer Vegetables, 124–25

Mediterranean Quinoa Salad, 120–21
Pancake Mix, 165
Purple Rice, 132–33
Steel-Cut Oatmeal with Dates, 26–27
Yummy Strawberry Yogurt Parfait, 18–19
Grandma's Spaghetti Gravy, 77–78
Great Pacific Garbage Patch, 38
Greek Shrimp with Feta, 88–89
Green Salad with Pears, Walnuts, and Feta, 131
Grilled Cheese with Nutella, 34, 35–36
Grocery shopping
    buying local foods. See Locavores
    Fair Trade Certified foods and, 172
    planning ahead, 8, 123
    reading labels, 2, 70
    shopping smart, 2
    smart alternatives to. See Farmer's market; Locavores

**H**

Harvesting for students, 107
Helping others
    cooking for a family in crisis, 78
    homeless people, 73
    recipe for action, 33
Homeless, helping, 73
Honey, measuring, 105
Hot Cocoa Mix, 171–73
Hummus, 168

**I**

Ingredients
    buying wisely. See Farmer's market; Grocery shopping; Locavores
    stocking pantry, 9
Invisible ink recipe, 160
Israeli Couscous Salad with Summer Vegetables, 124–25

**K**

Kale
    Kale Chips, 111
    Minestrone with White Beans and Kale, 71–72
Kids in kitchen, 5–12
    age appropriateness of recipes, 8

benefits of, 7
cleanliness considerations, 175
dessert dilemma, 12
hiding vegetables kids and, 9
improving nutrition of kids and, 9
involving, to save time, 8
joy of cooking with, 7
palate-pleasing foods (beyond treats), 7
reasons for, 7
Recipe for Cooking with Toddlers, 10–11
safety lesson, 175
timesavers for, 8–9
tips for teachers, 174–75
tools for, 6–7
unplugging unused appliances, 25
using recipes in this book with, 8
Knives, 6

**L**

Labels, reading and understanding, 2, 70, 172
Lemon
    Lemon Buttermilk Sherbet, 141–42
    Luscious Lemon Curd Tartlets, 158–59
Locavores
    buying local, 2, 17, 23
    canning foods, 4
    Community Supported Agriculture (CSA) and, 3
    defined, 2
    eating out and, 4
    farmer's market and, 2, 3
    field trips to introduce idea of, 4
    harvesting for students, 107
    helping family think like, 3–4
    planting something, 3. See also Gardening
    raising children as, 2–4
Lunch, 39–66
    A-B-C Frittata, 40–41
    Chewy Maple Granola Bars, 61–62
    Chinese Chicken Salad, 53–54
    Croque Monsieur, 58
    R & B Chili, 56–57
    Salty Pretzel Pillows, 63–66
    Smashed Avocado on Toast, 52
    Squashed Sweet Potato Soup, 45–46
    Thai Spring Rolls, 49–51
    There's Turkey in My Pocket, 55

Wrap It Up: BBQ Style, 44
Wrap It Up: L'egg-o Style, 48
Wrap It Up: Toga Style, 60
Luscious Lemon Curd Tartlets, 137–38

**M**

Making your own, 162–73
    Butter, 163–64
    Fresh Basil Pesto, 166–67
    Hot Cocoa Mix, 171–73
    Hummus, 168
    Pancake Mix, 165
    Puréed Pumpkin, 169–70
    Spice Rub Mix, 170
Mashed Sweet Potatoes with Caramelized Apples, 128–29
Measuring honey, 105
Meat. See also specific meats
    Meatless Monday and, 54
    pastured, 59
    sustainable farms and, 76
Meatless Monday, 54
Mediterranean Quinoa Salad, 120–21
Minestrone with White Beans and Kale, 71–72
Mini Frittatas, 14
Mini-muffin tins, 6
Miso-Glazed Salmon, 103
Mushrooms, in Summertime Kabobs with Udon Noodles, 90–93

**N**

Napkins, recyclable, 129
Nuts and seeds
    about: saving pumpkin seeds, 169
    Chewy Maple Granola Bars, 61–62
    Crunchy Granola, 37–38
    Grilled Cheese with Nutella, 34, 35–36
    Nutella Lace Cookies, 161

**O**

One-pot meals, 8
Oven-Fried Zucchini Sticks, 122–23

**P**

Pacific Ocean, garbage in, 38
Pancake Mix, 165

Pantry, stocking. *See also* Grocery shopping
Pasta and noodles
    Chicken Picatta with Linguine, 68–69
    Pumpkin Ravioli, 101–2
    Summertime Kabobs with Udon Noodles, 90–93
    Thai Spring Rolls, 49–51
    Wish-for-a-Fish Pasta, 82
Pastry brushes, 6
Pastured meat, 59
Pastured poultry, 70
Patriotic Fruit Salad, 126
Peaches
    Patriotic Fruit Salad, 126
    Peaches and Cream Cobbler, 144–46
    Simple Summer Frozen Yogurt, 143
Pears
    Cinnamon Pear Clafouti, 148
    Green Salad with Pears, Walnuts, and Feta, 131
Peppers
    about: cutting hot, 95; as fruits or vegetables, 52; hot and spicy, 95
    R & B Chili, 56–57
    Taco Salad, 94–95
Pest control, 89, 149
Pizza, Breakfast Anytime, 15–17
Planning ahead, 8, 123
Planting something. *See* Gardening
Plastic knives, 6
Pork
    about: pastured meat, 59
    A-B-C Frittata, 40–41
    Croque Monsieur, 58
    Pork Chops with Sage Butter, 84–85
    Pork Ribs with Asian BBQ Sauce, 74–75
    Sweet and Salty Glazed Bacon, 21
Potatoes
    Breakfast Anytime Pizza, 15–17
    Potato Latkes, 112–13
Pretzel-Coated Chicken, 108–9
Pretzel Pillows, Salty, 63–66
Pumpkins
    about: carving knives for, 6; as fruits or vegetables, 52; saving seeds, 169

Chocolate Chip Pumpkin Bread, 151–52
Pumpkin Ravioli, 101–2
Puréed Pumpkin, 169–70
Puréed Pumpkin, 169–70
Purple Rice, 132–33

**Q**

Quinoa, in Mediterranean Quinoa Salad, 120–21

**R**

R & B Chili, 56–57
Rainbow, eating colors of, 133
Raisins, in Carrot-Raisin Salad, 114–15
Raspberries. *See* Berries
Recipes. *See also specific recipes*
    about: overview of, 8
    age appropriateness of, 8
    for Cooking with Toddlers, 10–11
    using, with kids, 8
Resources, conserving, 60. *See also* Environmental awareness issues
Rice
    Acorn Squash and Wild Rice Bowls, 96–97
    Purple Rice, 132–33
Roasted Asparagus, 117
Roasted Broccoli with Lemon, 130
Roasting vs. baking, 153
Rotary cheese grater, 6

**S**

Safety lesson, 175
Sage Butter, 84–85
Salads
    Carrot-Raisin Salad, 114–15
    Chinese Chicken Salad, 53–54
    Couscous Salad with Apricots, Ginger, and Pine Nuts, 116
    Green Salad with Pears, Walnuts, and Feta, 131
    Mediterranean Quinoa Salad, 120–21
    Patriotic Fruit Salad, 126
    Taco Salad, 94–95
Salty Pretzel Pillows, 63–66
Sandwiches and wraps
    about: tortillas for wraps, 60; using what you have for, 44, 48; varying wraps for, 60

Croque Monsieur, 58
Grilled Cheese with Nutella, 34, 35–36
There's Turkey in My Pocket, 55
Wrap It Up: BBQ Style, 44
Wrap It Up: L'egg-o Style, 48
Wrap It Up: Toga Style, 60
Sauces and dressings
    Asian Dipping Sauces, 104–5
    Fresh Basil Pesto, 166–67
    Garlic Aioli, 118–19
    Grandma's Spaghetti Gravy, 77–78
    Mediterranean Quinoa Salad Dressing, 120–21
    Sage Butter, 84–85
    Sorrel Sauce, 86–87
    Vanilla Sauce, 148–49
Scissors, 7
Scoops, 6
Side dishes, 110–35
    Carrot-Raisin Salad, 114–15
    Couscous Salad with Apricots, Ginger, and Pine Nuts, 116
    Green Salad with Pears, Walnuts, and Feta, 131
    Israeli Couscous Salad with Summer Vegetables, 124–25
    Kale Chips, 111
    Lemon-Grilled Artichokes with Garlic Aioli, 118–19
    Mashed Sweet Potatoes with Caramelized Apples, 128–29
    Mediterranean Quinoa Salad, 120–21
    Oven-Fried Zucchini Sticks, 122–23
    Patriotic Fruit Salad, 126
    Potato Latkes, 112–13
    Purple Rice, 132–33
    Roasted Asparagus, 117
    Roasted Broccoli with Lemon, 130
    Spaghetti Squash Two Ways, 127
    Step-on-the-Gas Baked Beans, 134–35
Silicone pastry brushes, 6
Silicone spatulas, 6
Simple Summer Frozen Yogurt, 144
Simplifying preparations, 9
Slow cookers, 9
Smashed Avocado on Toast, 52
Smell and taste senses, 168
Soil. *See also* Gardening
    composting, 47
    worms and, 119

Sorrel-icious Sole, 86–87
Soups and stews
    Minestrone with White Beans and
        Kale, 71–72
    R & B Chili, 56–57
    Squashed Sweet Potato Soup,
        45–46
Spaghetti Squash Two Ways, 127
Spatulas, 6
Spice Rub Mix, 170
Spring gardening, 87
Spring Rolls, Thai, 49–51
Squash
    about: as fruits or vegetables, 52
    Acorn Squash and Wild Rice
        Bowls, 96–97
    Oven-Fried Zucchini Sticks,
        122–23
    Spaghetti Squash Two Ways, 127
    Squashed Sweet Potato Soup,
        45–46
    Summertime Kabobs with Udon
        Noodles, 90–93
Steel-Cut Oatmeal with Dates,
    26–27
Step-on-the-Gas Baked Beans,
    134–35
Stick 'em Up: Frozen Choco Bananas,
    137–38
Stocking pantry, 9
Strawberries. See Berries
Sugar shakers, 7
Summer gardening, 89
Summertime Kabobs with Udon
    Noodles, 90–93
Sustainable farms, 76
Sweet and Crunchy Strawberry Cups,
    139–40
Sweet and Salty Glazed Bacon, 21
Sweet potatoes
    Falling for Fall Quesadillas, 98–99
    Mashed Sweet Potatoes with
        Caramelized Apples, 128–29
    Sweet Potato Biscuits, 28–29

T

Taco Salad, 94–95
Taste and smell senses, 168
Thai Spring Rolls, 49–51
There's Turkey in My Pocket, 55
Timesavers, 8–9
Toddlers, Recipe for Cooking with,
    10–11

Tofu
    about: Meatless Monday and, 54
    Crispy Tofu Triangles with Asian
        Dipping Sauce, 104–5
    Summertime Kabobs with Udon
        Noodles, 90–93
    Thai Spring Rolls, 49–51
    Wrap It Up: BBQ Style, 44
Tomatoes, as fruits or vegetables, 52
Tools, for kids in kitchen, 6–7
Trash, in Pacific Ocean, 38
Treats, 136–61
    about: balancing other foods with,
        12; dilemma of, 12; palate-
        pleasing foods beyond, 7;
        pastry brushes and, 6
    Apple Crisp with Vanilla Sauce,
        148–49
    Cherry Chocolate Chip Cookies,
        154–55
    Chocolate Chip Pumpkin Bread,
        150–51
    Cinnamon Pear Clafouti, 147
    Coconut Macaroons, 152–53
    Flourless Chocolate Cake, 156–57
    Hot Cocoa Mix, 171–73
    Lemon Buttermilk Sherbet, 141–42
    Luscious Lemon Curd Tartlets,
        158–59
    Nutella Lace Cookies, 161
    Peaches and Cream Cobbler,
        144–45
    Simple Summer Frozen Yogurt,
        143
    Stick 'em Up: Frozen Choco
        Bananas, 137–38
    Sweet and Crunchy Strawberry
        Cups, 139–40
    Whipped Cream for, 140
Turkey
    Grandma's Spaghetti Gravy, 77–78
    Taco Salad, 94–95
    There's Turkey in My Pocket, 55
    Turkey Toes, 106–7
    Wrap It Up: BBQ Style, 44

V

Vanilla Sauce, 148–49
Vegetables. See also Salads; specific
    vegetables
    about: balancing desserts and, 12;
        foods as fruits or, 52; hiding, for
        kids, 9

Summertime Kabobs with Udon
    Noodles, 90–93
Thai Spring Rolls, 49–51
Vegetarianism, Meatless Monday
    and, 54
Volunteering. See Helping others

W

Watermelon, seedless, 146
Whey, 164
Whipped Cream, 141
Winter gardening, 115
Wish-for-a-Fish Pasta, 82
Worms, 119
Wraps. See Sandwiches and wraps

Y

Yogurt
    Banana Sunshine Smoothie, 20
    Simple Summer Frozen Yogurt,
        143
    Yummy Strawberry Yogurt Parfait,
        18–19
Yummy Strawberry Yogurt Parfait,
    18–19

Z

Zucchini. See Squash

**MICHELLE STERN** owns What's Cooking, a certified green company that offers cooking classes for children in the San Francisco Bay Area. Not only do her classes teach kids and their families to enjoy delicious homemade foods, but they also motivate families to use food and cooking to help those less fortunate. Her involvement with the International Association of Culinary Professionals and local school lunch reform led to an invitation to the White House, where Michelle participated in the launch of Michelle Obama's Chefs Move to Schools initiative. She has appeared on ABC's *View From the Bay* seven times and was recently a guest on a radio show about childhood obesity. In addition, her blog won the 2010 Parent & Child Green Blog Award from Scholastic. In her former life (pre-mommyhood), Michelle was a high school biology and environmental science teacher. Her teaching roots and eco-friendly mindset shine through in her current work with children. When she isn't in the kitchen, at the farmer's market, or at the computer, Michelle is the head chauffeur for her two children, dog walker to her two mutts, and chicken feeder for her backyard flock.